# The Face of China

C. H. Graves: Manchu woman with servant, 1902.

The Face of

# CHINA

## As Seen by Photographers & Travelers

# 1860-1912

### Preface by L. Carrington Goodrich
### Historical Commentary by Nigel Cameron

Photographs from the archives of
Arnold Arboretum, Harvard University
Bibliothèque Nationale; British Museum
Museum of Fine Arts, Boston
Essex Institute; Freer Gallery of Art
George Eastman House; Library of Congress
Museum of New Mexico; National Archives
National Army Museum
Naval Historical Center

New York Public Library
Peabody Museum of Salem
Smithsonian Institution
Victoria & Albert Museum
and the collections of
Chaoying Fang; Arnold H. Crane
Edmonton Art Gallery; Elaine Ellman
Graphics International; Hillelson/Kahn
Howard Ricketts; Daniel Wolf.

## An Aperture Book

*The Face of China As Seen by Photographers & Travelers 1860–1912 is an exhibition presented by the Philadelphia Museum of Art from April 15 to June 25, 1978. Thereafter the exhibition will be presented at the St. Louis Art Museum; the Cleveland Museum of Art; the Fine Arts Gallery, San Diego; and the Art Museum, University of California, Berkeley.*

*The Face of China, An Aperture Book, is published as a catalogue for the exhibition and as a book for general distribution. The picture research is by Carole Kismaric, and the editorial research is by Kate Morgan. The exhibition is coordinated by Lynn Kaufmann. The exhibition and publication are directed by Michael Hoffman.*

*Marvin Israel conceived a handsome book design, and this volume is richer and more vibrant because of his contribution.*

*Fred W. Drake, Associate Professor of History, University of Massachusetts, a China scholar who has an abiding interest in the early photographs of China, has provided the research for the captions and has benefited the project through insightful comment and careful scholarship.*

*Aperture, Inc., publishes a periodical, portfolios and books to communicate with serious photographers and creative people everywhere. A complete catalogue will be mailed upon request. Address: Millerton, New York 12546.*

*The Face of China is supported by a grant from the National Endowment for the Arts, Washington, D.C., a federal agency.*

 *Library of Congress Catalogue Card No.: 78-53932 ISBN: 0-89381-029-0 Cloth ISBN: 0-89381-032-0 Museum Edition*

*Composition by David E. Seham Associates, Metuchen, New Jersey. Printed by Rapoport Printing Corporation, New York City. Bound by Sendor Bindery, New York City. Manufactured in the United States of America.*

# Prelude to a New Era

In viewing this collection of photographs made during the final decades of the last dynasty, I am vividly reminded of my early years in China and of the life and culture of those days; much has vanished, some goes on as before.

Born in 1894, the Year of the Horse, in the shadow of the T'ung-chou Pagoda, I lived most of my early years, until 1911, in North China. I look back on this period as generally a pleasant one. In spite of what, to my parents and two older sisters, was a traumatic experience, I found the siege of Peking merely different and exciting, though I heartily disliked the food. I knew something was about to happen, in the spring of 1900, as thousands of Boxers foregathered in the outskirts of T'ung-chou; we could hear them at their drill and sometimes see them. For whipping his horse too severely, my eleven-year-old sister gave a tongue-lashing to a Boxer who happened to pass us on the sunken road by the North China Union College, where my father taught. He glared at her with astonishment but made no reply. When we and other Americans in our compound finally took off after midnight, early in June, in a string of Peking carts to make our way slowly up the old imperial highway ("good for ten years, bad for ten thousand," the Chinese say), I slept all the way in my mother's arms—hardly the act of a frightened child.

My earliest Chinese friends were my amah (we called her Chao *nai-nai*) and a boy of my age named Ta-lung ("Great Dragon"), the son of one of my father's colleagues. I liked the Chinese and Manchus with whom we were associated, and felt at ease with them. I learned how to fly a kite, touch off firecrackers, play with a diabolo, and kick a shuttlecock. I recall that we spent the summer of 1899 in the Western Hills, Hsi-shan, some twenty miles the other side of Peking. Sometimes, on a clear day, we could see that chain of hills beyond the massive walls encompassing the capital; the whole panorama was a lovely and unforgettable sight. From the year 1904 on, we spent our summers either at Pei-tai-ho (near a fishing village not far from the eastern terminus of the Great Wall) or at Chefoo (a port on the peninsula of Shantung), where I also went to school. So I learned to swim and became familiar with the life of the fishermen and the activities of a busy harbor. Once, in 1907, I sailed across to Port Arthur, in a junk manned by only three sailors, to see what the Japanese had done to capture "203 Meter Hill" from the Russians. Only two or three years earlier, when the wind was right, we used to hear the cannonading of the two contending forces, as each fought for mastery.

In 1905 my family moved to Peking, to a house on Yen-tai-hsieh chieh (Crooked Tobacco Pouch Street) near the Drum and Bell Towers, which used to boom out the time every two hours at night for the change of the watch. Several memories stick with me from those years: the delights of buying forbidden sweetmeats molded into rooster shapes, a dab of honey inside; skating on the imperial lake back of our house; coasting on ice boats on the moat north of the city wall; riding a bicycle out to the Great Bell Monastery or the Five Pagoda Temple.

One special occasion, in 1908, followed the death of both the emperor and his imperious aunt, the Empress Dowager. In preparation for the grand funeral of these two august figures, they covered the broad street that ran by our house with yellow earth over which the corteges were to pass, and fashioned a large number of imitation servitors — life-size, with real clothes, hair and headgear — to store in the Drum and Bell Towers against the day when they would be borne in state, then burned at the funeral. About the same time, and along the same street, Prince Ch'un, as regent and father of Heir Apparent Pu-yi, had to proceed at a brisk pace in a special carriage, surrounded by outriders, to the rear gate of the Forbidden City for an early-morning audience with the court high ministers. Every shop along the way was shuttered, and civilians were ordered to keep out of sight. This was a temptation. With another American boy, I sneaked up to the third story of our house before dawn to have a look; inevitably, we were spotted by a watchful guard and given a severe talking-to.

Finally, in January 1911, when the pneumonic plague then in Manchuria threatened to reach Peking, we traveled by the newly built railroad to Hankow, and then by steamer down the Yangtze to Nanking for a few days before continuing on to Shanghai. For the first time, I became acquainted with part of that great river system. Only years later did I make my way up the rapids and gorges to the border of Szechwan, and down to Changsha on the Hsiang River, and to Canton. I was fortunate. In my twenty years in China as boy and man, I visited fourteen of its eighteen provinces and, in addition, the southern part of Manchuria as well as Korea and Japan.

The nineteenth century is not one of China's great moments in history. The successors of Nurhachi (1559–1626), the first Manchu to sit on the Dragon Throne, lacked the capacity for government of such ancestors as K'ang-hsi (r. 1662–1722) and Ch'ien-lung (r. 1736–95). The relative prosperity of the eighteenth century rapidly gave way to increasing poverty among the masses consequent upon the remarkable explosion of the population. From an estimated number of 150 million in 1700, the figure jumped in 1800 to over 300 million and by 1850 had passed 400 million. People on the southwest coast drifted to Taiwan, Hainan, and southeastern Asia; people in the north, to Manchuria; people in the lower Yangtze valley, to the western reaches of the river. Some were even enticed to migrate to North America and South Africa. Land owners in the center and south seized the opportunity to prey on their tenants, who were in turn exploited by usurers.

The unhappiness of the peasantry showed in incipient rebellions. Secret societies, age-old in some instances, proved difficult for imperial forces to control. The White Lotus Rebellion (1796–1804) was followed by piracy on the southeast coast. The Taiping outburst, which started mid-century in south China and spread to the north, was suppressed only in 1864 — "one of the greatest civil wars in world history." Moslem uprisings broke out in the northwest and Yunnan province in the southwest, and the massive Nien Rebellion disrupted northern China. All this meant a severe drain on the finances and military strength of the government, which had to face at the same time the British insistence on trading in opium. When in March 1839 the imperial commissioner impounded and destroyed more than 20,000 chests of that drug, war began and did not end until three years later.

The treaty that ensued opened five ports to trade—until then only Macao and Canton were accessible to foreign shippers—and ceded Hong Kong to the British. Anti-foreign activity was the predictable result. The French joined forces with the British in several skirmishes that led to the fall of Canton, after which the combined fleet sailed north to Tientsin to conclude treaties with the Manchu government. (The Russian and American diplomats, without firing a shot, gained equivalent advantages as signatories.) Still not satisfied, the British and French wanted to sign the treaties in the capital. On their arrival in 1859 at the mouth of the Pei-ho, the guns of the Taku fort repelled them. During the next year, however, Ambassadors Lord Elgin and Baron Gros, with some 20,000 troops (including a Cantonese corps of 2,500!), succeeded in fighting their way upriver to the vicinity of Peking, sacking the Yüan-ming Yüan and other palatial structures of the Manchu emperors and forcing the ratification of the 1858 treaties in Peking. Now, for the first time in China's long history, diplomatic representatives of foreign powers were allowed to reside in the capital—a grave blow to imperial prestige. After decades of lost wars, the final calamity began in 1898: an anti-foreign uprising, originating in the eastern province of Shantung, by the I-hoch'üan (the Boxers). This group, joined in 1900 by the imperial troops, sought to exterminate the foreign communities in Tientsin and the French cathedral in Peking, only to be defeated in August of that year by an international army including the British, French, Russians, Japanese, and Americans.

Aside from the shocks in mainland China, there were setbacks of control on the periphery: the loss of Taiwan and the Pescadores to Japan, and the freedom from tribute-bearing status of Korea, Liu-ch'iu (the Ryukyu Islands), Vietnam, Nepal, Tibet, and Burma. Only eastern Turkestan, long a corridor for Chinese traffic to the West, was maintained (and in 1884 designated as the province of Sinkiang).

Meanwhile, much of Chinese life went on as before. Great junks still sailed up from the south around the Shantung peninsula to Niuchuang in Manchuria; other craft, twenty to thirty meters in length and with up to 500 ton burden, sailed to the entrance of the Grand Canal on the Yangtze; by the year 1884, according to one observer, each of the ports of Ningpo, Foochow and Amoy counted 700 to 800 ocean-going vessels. Fishing smacks by the thousand made their daily excursions along the coast to supply the markets from Canton to Mukden, and possibly even a greater number plied the rivers and canals. The dread passage up the middle Yangtze, through the Gorges, was effected with the aid of naked trackers who hauled the vessels past dangerous rocks and over shoals. Other boat people, in the quieter waters of the Pearl River estuary, spent their entire lives on board, cooking their meals, bearing children, and trafficking with those on shore. Pleasure boats, too, were available for those of the leisure class who wanted to spend a few quiet days coasting through the canals and streams and lakes of a picturesque backwater. The Grand Canal for the most part was kept in operation, and rice-laden boats helped stock the capital's great granaries. In the upper reaches of the Hwang-ho, rafts buoyed by inflated pigskins navigated the shallow water.

People still, like the folk in Chaucer's day, continued to "goon on pilgrimages": to the five sacred mountains—T'ai in the east, Hua in the west, Heng in the north, Heng (a different character) in the south and Chung in central China—and to the holy places of Buddhism. Some went in style, by cart and boat and sedan chair, others on foot (even bound feet), and by successive prostrations.

The examination system meant for many boys not only intensive study in literature and handwriting, but also travel to the subprefectural or prefectural city for the first test and, if they passed, to the provincial capital for the second. This was a test that lasted a week or so. Here a great winnowing took place, for only the best were permitted to proceed to Peking for the final, actually two, examinations. Thousands made the trip every triennium, but only 300 or so were awarded degrees. Failure must have been a traumatic experience for the great majority, for not only they but their families, who had supported them for sixteen to twenty years, depended on their success; the accolade of a *chin-shih* degree meant a place in the official hierarchy and appointments generally for life, either in the provinces or at the capital. Nonetheless, the series of events in spite of the trauma, must have been enriching. Many had never traveled before, and few had tasted the delights of Peking—its theaters and grog shops, its night life, its display of grandeur and power. Then, too, there was the encounter with some of the best young minds of China—future poets, essayists, painters and calligraphers, some of whom they might well meet again officially or socially.

As the years went on, certain perspicacious Chinese saw that Japan was progressing at a faster rate than China in the effort to resist foreign encroachment. The reason was obvious: the Japanese were welcoming foreign advisers, sending select students abroad and to a limited degree introducing foreign education. Subsequent to the opening of the treaty ports in 1842, Protestant missionaries, both British and American, tentatively initiated Western-type schools which developed into colleges of a more advanced level. After diplomatic relations were established with the treaty powers in 1860, the need to train official interpreters became obvious; hence the foundation in 1862 of the T'ung-wen kuan in Peking, with auxiliary schools at Canton and Shanghai. There followed in short order a school for mechanical engineering and a college for naval students, both on the southeast coast. Whereas the Japanese had selected Germany as the country most suited for the training of their elite, the Chinese decided first on the United States and in the 1870's dispatched 120 boys in four contingents to New England. Most of them returned to perform usefully as engineers, railroad directors, naval officers, diplomatic aides, newspaper editors, teachers, telegraph operators, medical doctors and the like. In 1876 the government dispatched another thirty to England and France. So, through the influence of Britain, France and America, did Western education begin to seep into China—not only Western ideas and literature, but also science, music, and games.

Despite the growing accent on Westernization, critical scholarship of the older sort continued. Revised gazetteers were produced in almost every district and prefecture and province. Collections of important works were compiled and printed; catalogs of all sorts were prepared; a number of old books were rediscovered. Chinese newspapers began to circulate in Hong Kong (1855) and Shanghai (1861), and a significant piece of fiction, *The Adventures of Lao Ts'an*, appeared at the end of the century in a Chinese daily published in Tientsin.

China is a land of farms—for cotton

and tobacco, for rice, wheat, barley, sorghum, cabbage, bamboo sprouts, lotus roots and almost every vegetable one can think of, and groves of oranges, persimmons, pears and other fruits. This produce had to be transported to market when it was ripe, and at a very early hour, since there was no adequate way to keep it fresh for any length of time. Thus a town or city market at dawn was a busy place indeed. "The congested condition," observed one spectator, "with the great variety of vegetables, makes it almost as impressive a sight as Billingsgate market in London." Mixed with the hubbub of haggling between buyer and seller is the squeak of the oncoming wheelbarrows, often with a load of two pigs strapped on either side, each adding its voice to the din. And there are live chickens and ducks in openwork baskets, and fish in open tubs.

China is also a land of mines. As far back as the third century before our era, the government was monopolizing salt and iron: salt from the seashore and from the deposits in Shansi and Szechwan, iron from scattered areas all over China. Coal was extracted from areas in the north, northwest and southwest. Having once seen them, one will never forget the long strings of Bactrian camels, burdened with bags of coal and lime, wending their

way into such centers as Peking, or the huge windmills operating in the salterns north of Tientsin and near the mouth of the Yangtze.

Proceeding across the face of China, one seems to find almost everyone perpetually at work: women tending their silkworms and helping out with farm chores, their daughters caring for the young fry; small boys minding water buffaloes; men shoeing horses, or manufacturing paper in the sunshine, or hauling in their nets of fish by the seaside, or fashioning porcelain bowls; soldiers drilling; groups of laborers wielding ropes for tamping the earth; Taoist priests and Buddhist monks overseeing funeral processions; shopkeepers bending over an abacus. The list is endless; the Chinese countryside is a busy place.

But the time comes when all toil must cease, when workers may relax and enjoy long-untasted meat and drink. This is New Year's, when the first new moon becomes apparent. Over the lintels of many doors appear such sentiments as "May Heaven send down the five blessings" — wealth, posterity, long life, absence of pain, and no sickness. In the final week of the year, the picture of the kitchen god is removed, his mouth smeared with sweetmeats and his image ceremonially burned to ensure that he will

have only good to report to the Jade Emperor. At dawn on New Year's Day he will return in a new picture, in a niche over the kitchen stove, to supervise family affairs for the ensuing twelve or thirteen months. Strings of firecrackers are fired to announce the approach of the year and to frighten away evil spirits. When possible, all members of the family join under the parental roof to share in the celebration, and for fifteen days no real business is transacted. It is a time for joy and renewal.

L. Carrington Goodrich
Dean Lung Professor Emeritus
of Chinese, Columbia University

The Face of China – Photographers & Travelers

*The empire of China is, in a manner, separated from all the rest of the world; situated in a fine and healthy climate, surrounded by the ocean to the east and south, by a chain of . . . barren mountains on the north and west, along which runs the famous wall as an additional defence. But what, in my opinion is a greater security to the empire against invaders . . . is the barren desert . . . for several hundred miles westward . . . which scarce any regular army can pass. . . .*

*What part of China I saw is mostly plain, interspersed with hills and rising grounds. The whole is pleasant and well cultivated, producing wheat and other grain, together with abundance of cattle and poultry.*

*Besides the necessaries, the Chinese have also many of the superfluities of life; particularly, fine fruits . . . likewise mines of gold, silver, copper, lead and iron. . . .*

*Silks are the common dress, of the better sort of people, of both sexes, and coarse cotton-cloth that of the lower classes. . . .*

*The Chinese are a civilized and hospitable people; complaisant to strangers, and to one another; very regular in their manners and behaviour, and respectful to their superiors; but above all their regard for their parents, and decent treatment of their women of all ranks, ought to be imitated, and deserve great praise. These good qualities are a natural consequence of the sobriety, and uniformity of life, to which they have long been accustomed.    John Bell*

*My design . . . is to present a series of pictures of China and its people. Such as shall convey an accurate impression of the country as well as of the arts, usages, and manners which prevail in different provinces of the Empire. With this intention I made the camera the constant companion of my wanderings. . . . I . . . frequently enjoyed the reputation of being a dangerous geomancer, and my camera was held to be a dark mysterious instrument which, combined with my naturally, or supernaturally, intensified eyesight gave me power to see through rocks and mountains, to pierce the very souls of the people and to produce miraculous pictures by some black art. . . .    John Thomson*

E. H. Wilson: Buddhist shrine at Shih-pao-chai, Szechwan, on Yangtze River, January 5, 1909.
The pagoda and building atop the rock undoubtedly attracted pilgrims from afar.

14    Photographer unknown: Monastery, Orphan Island, Yangtze River, c1875.

Photographer unknown: Ruins of a Buddhist temple near Sian, capital of Shensi, c1900.

15

Felice A. Beato: Interior, coastal fort near Tientsin, captured during Second Opium War, August 1860.
The Anglo-French campaign ended with the invasion of Peking and a new set of unequal treaties.

Thomas Childe: Ruins of Yüan-ming Yüan, Old Summer Palace northwest of Peking, c1875. These European-style buildings were designed in the eighteenth century by the Jesuit Giuseppe Castiglione. In 1860 British and French forces, at the direction of Lord Elgin, burned the palace in retaliation for mistreatment of prisoners of war.

John Thomson: The arsenal at Nanking, c1868. One of the first of its kind in China, the arsenal manufactured hundreds of tons of guns and ammunition yearly with money from provincial sources and from duties on Western goods.

Photographer unknown: Wu-t'ai-shan, Shansi, c1900.

John Thomson: Prince K'ung (I-hsien), leader of the reform movement after 1860, c1868.

Attributed to Thomas Childe: The Great Wall, c1877. Originally built along the northern frontier by China's first unifier, Ch'in Shih Huang-ti, after 221 B.C., the Great Wall symbolized for many Westerners an attempt to restrict foreign influence. Rebuilt during the fifteenth century to extend some 2,000 miles, it proved more effective as a geographical boundary.

22

Thomas Childe: Old Summer Palace, Yu-chuan Shan, Jade Spring Hill, c1877.

24    Photographer unknown: Lily pond in garden of South China, c1860.

*(June 4, 1869) The little cuckoo is heard on all sides, day and night. Its strange cry can be represented fairly exactly by the following notes:*

*(January 16, 1869) The trees I see today are the lancelolate pine, a cypress with large cones, a large spiny Aralia, the Platanus, Liguidambas, alder and hemp palm, the latter very abundant and in fruit. . . . There are many birds today. I flush several ring-neck pheasants but do not follow them. I kill my first specimens of a new bird, a kind of Garrulax or trochalopteron with green wings and tail and white iris. . . . The young pupils of the college also amuse themselves by catching birds with a silk net which they hang vertically on bamboo trees. They bring me their prey, consisting of Leiothrix Lutea and an Abrovnis with a fawn-colored face.     Abbé David*

*Verdant trees and yellow canaries, mountains are everywhere.*
*Aimlessly I return from the stream after watching the clouds.*
*In life, one is not allowed to be always free,*
*An infrequent chance to visit the mountains—this is leisure.     Hsü Pen*

*Filling the valleys are shadows of spring; lining the stream green moss.*
*Only where violet mists arise are there clefts in the cliffs.*
*A boy of the mountains, with an urgent message, knocks at the gate:*
*He comes with a poem by his master, asking for a painting in exchange.     Kao Ch'i*

*We passed up a stone walk covered with a roof of translucent sea shells to a central temple stacked with boards used in making seats and tables required in the examinations. From this temple, walks lead to the twelve thousand individual cells in which the students are locked for the two days and night allotted for the completion of their essays or poems; for the examinations are on literature and not on the sciences. These cells are only about five and one-half by four feet—rather cramped quarters in which to spend forty-eight continuous hours.     George W. Caldwell, M.D.*

*I had been taught the Confucian Analects and had been constantly trained how to behave like a "superior man," so I walked with my eyes looking straight ahead. Even the rustling of my new blue satin gown seemed to disturb the silence and made me walk slower. Having since then visited Western cathedrals I can imagine now what our two figures looked like, the little nun's and mine, moving slowly through the vast halls.     Chiang Yee*

*Weighing all the good and bad qualities of the respective nations in an impartial scale, we do not hesitate to award to the Chinese the palm of superiority above all other Asiatics; but comparing the whole mass with the inhabitants of Europe in the present age, we look up with veneration to the spirit of improvement which has constituted the latter the empires of the world. Once they were on a par, they even fell beneath the Chinese; but now they have risen to a height almost to dazzle the Asiatic eye.     Reverend Karl Gützlaff*

Photographer unknown: Examination halls, with 7,500 cells, Canton, c1873. One of the centers of periodic examinations administered by the government. Few examinees managed to pass through the highly competitive, grueling process that led to bureaucratic power. It was here that the leader of the Taiping Rebellion, Hung Hsiu-ch'üan, failed his examinations.

Joseph F. Rock: Mosque of old-sect Mohammedans in walled city of T'ao-chou, Kansu,
28   July 19, 1925. Large numbers of Chinese Moslems inhabited the province of Kansu.

Felice A. Beato: View from An-ting Gate, located on the eastern portion of the north wall of Peking, October 21, 1860.

Felice A. Beato: French point of entry, North Fort, August 21, 1860.

M. A. Baptista (?): Priests and laymen at the grave of a long-dead Christian, Macao, c1860.

Felice A. Beato: Headquarters staff, Pei-t'ang Fort, August 1860. Against the British and French forces north of Taku, the Chinese defenders put up a strong fight, using lances, muskets, cannon (some made of wood bound with leather) and crossbows.

Felice A. Beato: The Great North Fort at Taku, at the mouth of the Pei-ho, August 21, 1860. After the surrender, the interior of the fort was strewn with Chinese dead. French scaling ladders are still in place. A Chinese crossbow lies atop a parapet.

33

Photographer unknown: Execution scene, c1860. Death by decapitation was considered one
of the less severe forms of capital punishment since the offender suffered only momentarily.

Photographer unknown: Ruins of Peking, 1900. Boxer "rebels" and imperial troops
attacked the section of Peking in which Western merchants and diplomats lived.

36        Felice A. Beato: North corner, Peking wall, October 1860.

E. H. Wilson: Criminals awaiting execution, 1899-1910. Tied to a cross-shaped frame, two criminals wait to be moved to the scene of their death. The queue was passed through a hole in the top of the vertical post to keep the body in position, and a rope around the neck was twisted until strangulation occurred.

*(The 21st Day. The middle of the hour shen. Aug. 15, 1900, 4 pm)*

*I have now received news that Grand Secretary Hsu-T'ung has committed suicide . . . his wife and four sons with their women folk have also committed suicide. Alas, never in all history has such strange misfortune been seen that the relatives of the Imperial Clan have fallen so low that their caps and robes fill the gutter!*

*If the people of the whole country together had shouldered the responsibility things would not have had such a poor out come. Grand Secretary Lu understood it well, when at the beginning he criticized the boxers' calamitous magic arts as not being worth a smile from a wise man. Indeed they are no more than the point of an autumn hair.*

*"The glory of spring has gone and does not return" (Yu-hsueh) For the servants of our great Ching dynasty nothing remains but to die. Yet it is strange that one's plans should be frustrated when Heaven and men were of one mind! My womenfolk all intend to commit suicide . . . as for myself, I do not think of such a thing.*

*All communication of news with the outside world is now interrupted and everywhere foreign robbers are looting. But the rumor goes that everybody's life is spared who puts up a white flag. Very likely the foreign barbarians will have no means of finding my hidden treasure and so I shall not move elsewhere but shall just quietly await things here. En-chu has disappeared, I do not know where he is. My servants have all gone to their homes, there is no one to prepare my evening . . . (These were his last words; later that night, Ching-shan was murdered by his eldest son.)* From The Diary of His Excellency Ching-Shan

*"In a week it will be my wedding day. Will you graciously grant me a few days' absence?"*

*"Of course. . . . But tell me, Chang, have you ever seen your bride?"*

*He looked at me in astonishment. . . . But the innate courtesy of the Chinese does not permit them to show how shocked they often are at the lack of decorum of foreigners. . . . Chang quickly recovered himself. "No, lady; she comes from the Eight Li Village outside Peking. My uncle arranged the marriage . . . and he assures me that the girl is young, just sixteen, and not ugly."*     Hope Danby

*The women of all ranks stay pretty much at home. The smallness of their feet, which renders them unable to walk any considerable distance, makes their confinement less disagreeable. As soon as a girl comes into the world, they bind her tender feet with tight bandages . . . to prevent their growing. This custom prevails universally, the Tartar Manchu ladies, residing in China, only excepted, who appear to have no inclination to conform to this fashion. . . .*     John Bell

*When I was nine they started to bind my feet again and they hurt so much that for two years I had to crawl on my hands and knees. Sometimes at night. . .I could not sleep. I stuck my feet under my mother and she lay on them so they hurt less and I could sleep. But by the time I was eleven my feet did not hurt and by the time I was thirteen they were finished. . . . My feet were very small indeed.*     Ning Lao T'ai-t'ai

*A young boy to his mother said:*
*Don't give me a bound-foot woman to wed!*
*Yesterday our teacher told us all*
*That bound-foot women are frail and dull.*

*They can't read words or understand books,*
*To the bedroom they confine their looks.*
*If with your son's wish you'll abide,*
*Please don't get me a foot-bound bride!*     Chia Shen

Keystone View Company: Chinese bride and groom, with servant, 1905.

42    Photographer unknown: Chinese courtesan (?), c1875.

Photographer unknown: Ceremonial sedan chair, c1875.                                                                43

Photographer unknown: Interior of Chinese home, c1875.

Photographer unknown: Wa Fung of Soochow and Woo Nu Quei of Canton, merchants in Shanghai, c1870.

John Thomson: Precious Cloud Pavilion, Longevity Hill, Old Summer Palace, c1868. A fine example of Chinese palace architecture, the pavilion was constructed on a base of white marble. The doors and windows are of bronze, the roof of ceramic tile.

Photographer unknown: Chinese family, c1875. Women of several generations of a
wealthy family sit before a moon gate in which calligraphic scrolls have been hung.

48    Photographer unknown: "The Dragon Tree," c1875.

(?) Miller: Chinese merchant's family, c1865.

49

H. C. White: Temple of Ah Ma, Macao, c1900. Situated at the base of Barra Hill, the shrine honors a poor Fukienese
girl who, according to legend, brought safely through a typhoon the only junk to grant her request for passage.

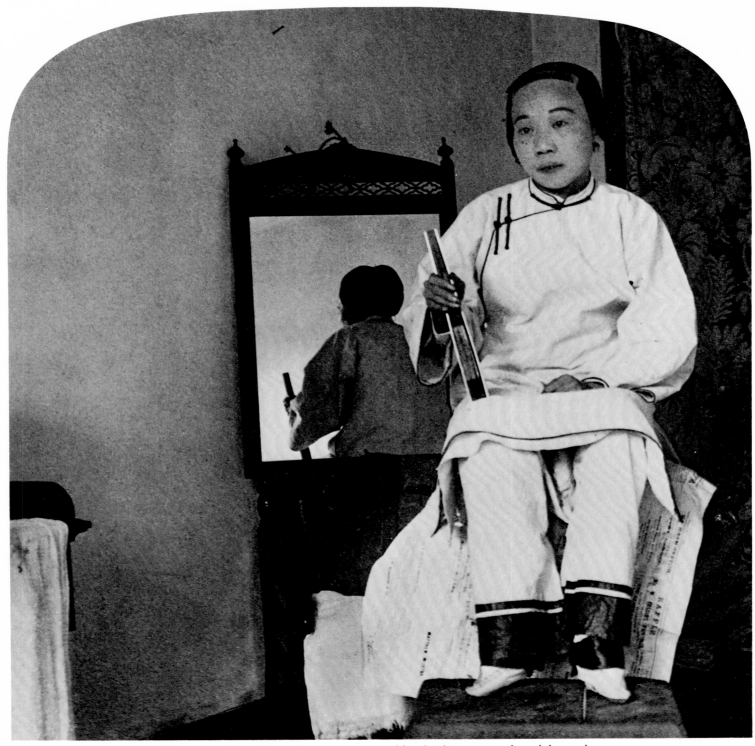

Underwood and Underwood: Woman with bound feet, 1900. The practice of foot-binding was popularized during the
Sung dynasty (960-1279) and is said to have been originated by a dancing girl in the court of the previous dynasty.

Photographer unknown: Probably the wife of Huang Tsan-t'ang, governor of Kwang-tung, 1862. The embroidered pheasant on the breast plaque of her official garb denotes her husband's high status in the second rank of the civil bureaucracy.

Photographer unknown: Five-storied pagoda built on wall of Canton, c1860.                                       53

Attributed to Princess Der Ling: Empress Dowager Tz'u-hsi, 1903. The Empress Dowager (1835-1908) poses in a scene that portrays her as the Buddhist Goddess of Mercy. Li Lien-ying, the notorious chief eunuch, is at the right.

*Tzu means "parental love." Hsi means "joy." Tzu Hsi is undoubtedly a remarkable woman. Besides having directed the destinies of China for twenty-seven years, without being in the least entitled to do so, she is said to be a brilliant artist, often giving away her pictures; and she also writes poetry. Some people suspect her of having been instrumental in causing the death of the Emperor Hien Feng, as also of his and her son Tung Chih. She is more than suspected of having caused the death of her sister, the mother of the Emperor Kwangshu. . . .     Mrs. Archibald Little*

*The people are as hard as steel. They are eaten up both soul and body, by the world. They don't seem to feel that here can be reality in anything beyond the senses. To them our doctrine is foolishness, our preaching contemptible, our talk jargon, our thoughts insanity, and our hopes and fears mere brain phantoms. . . . Think of the conversion of four hundred millions of the most proud, superstitious, and godless people of the human race. Sometimes I am ready to give up in despair and think that China is doomed to destruction, that to raise it out of its state of moral and spiritual degradation is a matter of impossibility.     From letter written in Shanghai by missionary Griffith John*

*After the gay crowds of Japanese women and children, the predominance of men in a Chinese crowd is a very marked feature; women are comparatively few, and all are large-footed — in other words, plebeian (none the worse for that in our eyes). But the ladies of the lily feet (i.e. the distorted hoofs) must remain in the seclusion of their homes, or at least must be carried through the streets in closely-covered chairs. Those we do see are very simply dressed in prune-coloured loosely-fitting clothes; but all have bare heads and black hair elaborately dressed and ornamented with clasps of imitation jadestone; most have earrings and bangles to match.*
*Constance F. Gordon-Cumming*

*The charm of travel in China is the unexpected. In Europe it is all cut and dried. . . . Now in China it is all the other way. There is no guide-book. You never know when you may arrive . . . you rarely know where a head wind may delay your boat, necessitating tying up for the night in some noisy, carousing village; or a favourable wind carry you before sunset to the quiet haven under a projecting cliff where you desired to be, in time to take a walk and discover a beautiful old temple, now crumbling to decay but commanding one of the world's most beautiful views and with quaint carvings on its gateways and stone lions guarding them, their heads on one side. . . . In land travel it is the same . . . you meet such strange things, a wedding-party, for instance, gaily caparisoned, going out to fetch the bride. As they wind down the mountainside with their flags flying you cannot but pause and watch.*
*Archibald Little*

Donald Mennie: Ha-ta-men Street, Peking, c1920.

店悟屏壽元饙    綢緞課科金

Photographer unknown: Ha-ta-men Street, from Ha-ta (or Ch'ung-wen) Gate on eastern side of south wall of Tartar City, Peking, c1865. Ha-ta-men Street led north from the Chinese City through the Tartar City, in which were located the palaces of Manchu princes, the residences of important Manchu families and the major government buildings.

Photographer unknown: The Seventh Prince, c1880.

Attributed to John Thomson: Chinese woman and servant, c1868.

John Thomson: Bridge over Han River at Ch'ao-chou, Fukien, c1868.

Reverend Harry Parsons: Secretary to Lo brothers, with copy of New Testament, c1920. As legal adviser and administrator of the Lo brothers estate, the secretary wielded considerable power in the community.

Reverend Harry Parsons: T'u-mu, one of the Lo brothers of Mao-mao-shan, c1920.

Felice A. Beato: Five-storied structure, Canton, April 1860.

John Thomson: Itinerant tradesmen, Kiukiang, Kiangsi, c1868. Left to right: a soup vendor,
a public scribe telling a woman's fortune, a barber and a wood turner with his customer.

65

John Thomson, c1868. (top left) Old Weng, a humble Manchu bannerman employed to watch a city gate in Peking. (top right) Bactrian camels carried brick tea to Mongolia, Siberia and Central Asia. (bottom left) People of Amoy, a treaty port in southeast Fukien. (bottom right) Military mandarins commonly traveled on horseback while civilian mandarins were carried in sedan chairs.

John Thomson, c1868. (top left) The peep show brought exotic wonders of the foreign world to the villages of China. (top right) The cotton-spinning machine was a rudimentary appliance driven by foot. (bottom left) A traveling chiropodist operates on a corn and dresses the toenails of a customer. (bottom right) The wheelbarrow was invented by the Chinese ten centuries before it appeared in the West.

Felice A. Beato: Nine-storied pagoda and Tartar Street, Canton, April 1860.

John Thomson: Physic Street, Canton c1868.

70    Felice A. Beato: View of Confucian temple from An-ting Gate, Peking, October 1860.

Photographer unknown: Old gentlemen of Canton dressed in summer clothing, 1861.

*Even a man riding the poorest little donkey, or a person occupying the most miserable of rickshaws, displays a certain amount of stateliness. I could not help laughing now and then when I saw seated on a wretched, meek little donkey a stout Chinaman, with the air of an emperor on his steed of ceremony.     Henri Borel*

*(March, 1866) "What is there to do in a shelter except dream?" says La Fontaine; and what is there to do on a mule except think? The good animal does not distract you; it walks along by itself at a steady pace. Just the same it would be dangerous to fall asleep on its back, for you would risk awakening in the dust as has happened several times to my young Chinese assistant, who has fallen off his docile mount. Thus I let my mind wander freely about divers objects which present themselves during the six hours of morning and six of afternoon that I am perched on my beast, when no one speaks to me. In China, silence is the rule while traveling.     Abbé David*

*The Chinese, who have been thought of as the most prosaic race in the world, are in some respects the most entertaining. It is the laughter-loving Chinese mind which took the sober, introspective Buddha of India and made of him the merry genie, Mi-Do [The Laughing Buddha].     Upton Close*

Underwood and Underwood: Rice paddies and tea shrubs in the hills of Kiangsi, Southeast China, 1902.

74    Photographer unknown: Boats on Yangtze River, c1870.

Photographer unknown: Peking, c1860.

76    E. H. Wilson: Countryside south of Ichang, western Hupei, January 20, 1909.

E. H. Wilson: Bamboo raft on Ya River, near Chia-ting, Szechwan, December 9, 1908.

77

Photographer unknown: Lung-men Buddhist cave temple near Loyang, c1910.

Photographer unknown: Westerners and Chinese at temple near Soochow, c1865.

John Thomson: Jui-lin, Manchu governor-general of Kwang-tung and Kwang-si, c1868.

Photographer unknown: Bridge, New Summer Palace, c1890.

82    Donald Mennie: Grand P'ai-lou, c1920. The marble entrance to the Ming tombs northwest of Peking.

Photographer unknown: Monks in private grotto, Peking, c1865.

Photographer unknown: Tomb near Foochow, c1865. The tomb of a wealthy family named K'ung
(the family name of Confucius), with the altar at which sacrifices to ancestors were made.

John Thomson: Buddhist monks, Ku-shan Monastery, Fukien, c1868. Known to
the Chinese as Bubbling Spring, the prosperous monastery supported 200 priests.

Thomas Childe: Astronomical observatory, Peking, c1877. Emperor K'ang-hsi's fascination with science and his support of
Jesuit Ferdinand Verbiest resulted in refitting the observatory with the latest instruments of the seventeenth century.

*If we understand their methods can we not expect that after a century or so we can reject the barbarians and stand on our own feet?     Li Hung-chang*

*Eastern learning has spirit as its point of departure; Western learning has matter as its point of departure.     Liang Ch'i-ch'ao*

*. . . the province of Kiangsu used to have a densely populated countryside, a village every half li, a marketplace or town every three li, smoking chimneys . . . everywhere, and chickens and dogs to be heard everywhere. Now we see nothing but weeds, briars, hazels obstructing the roads . . . no inhabitants for twenty or thirty li. Among broken walls and ruined buildings, one or two orphan children or widows survive out of hundreds of inhabitants. Their faces have no colour, and they groan while waiting for death. . . . As I, your official, am holding the post of Governor, my heart grows sick when I see these terrible conditions with my own eyes.     Li Hung-chang*

*A white barbarian may be in the Chinese world, but he never becomes of it. He may be an onlooker, an adviser . . . but he never becomes more than the utensil of the more cunning and sophisticated Chinese mind.      Upton Close*

*I have seen Li-Hung-Chang, and he wishes me to stay with him. I cannot desert China in her present crisis, and would be free to act as I think fit. I therefore beg to resign my commission in Her Majesty's service. . . .*

*The yellow jacket, which has been conferred on me, is a regular Chinese distinction, with which some twenty Mandarins have been decorated; it constitutes the recipient, one of the Emperor's body guards. I do not care two pence about these things, but know that you and my father like them.*
*From* Chinese Gordon: The Uncrowned King

*Gordon is now stationed temporarily at K'un-shan, and has stated that he is not subject to the control of Your official [Li Hung-chang]. As Your official's military strength is adequate for campaigning. . . . I hope that the Tsungli Yamen [Foreign Office] . . . will reach agreement on Gordon's retirement. . . .      Li Hung-chang*

Photographer unknown: Execution in Old Shanghai, September 1904. Major criminals were sometimes left to die publicly as an example to the innocent. A "cage" was constructed so that the inmate could either stand on tiptoe to relieve the pressure around his neck or finally suspend himself until he strangled.

90      Photographer unknown: Teatime, c1875.

Photographer unknown: Western businessmen in rattan factory, c1875. In the last decades of the Ch'ing dynasty impoverished and dispossessed Chinese peasants formed an enormous pool of cheap labor for work in factories.

92       Photographer unknown: A room in the dwelling of a wealthy Chinese family, Canton, c1870.

Photographer unknown: Banquet, c1920. Businessmen dine in a Western-style restaurant.
The place of honor, facing the door, is occupied by a Chinese and his Western counterpart.

94    Photographer unknown: Boat celebration of Duke of Edinburgh's arrival, Hong Kong, c1872.

Photographer unknown: Western woman and child, c1875. After the Treaty of Peking in 1860, Westerners were allowed to reside for the first time in Chinese communities beyond the treaty ports, gaining status and influence they had not ordinarily experienced in their own countries.

*We went on, and thus came near a very large Chinese house and garden, with a queer tale of a dead magician, where we had been hospitably entertained before. The people knew he had been a magician, because he used to disappear every day at a certain hour; and someone peeped through a crack one day, and saw him actually in a cold-water bath like a fish. I thought it would be a pleasure to visit the garden once more; but again a man shouting and gesticulating, this time armed with one of those heavy hoes they use in digging, which he brandished across my face! It seemed his master, who had entertained us, was dead, and this rustic would have no photography.      Mrs. Archibald Little*

*These two conversions filled me with great joy, as they were the first I had made. I may here take occasion to observe, that if our European missionaries in China would conduct themselves with less ostentation, and accommodate their manners to persons of all ranks and conditions, the number of converts would be immensely increased; for the Chinese possess excellent natural abilities, and are both prudent and docile. But unfortunately, our missionaries have adopted the lofty and pompous manner known in China by the apellation of "T'i-mien" [haughty]. Their garments are made of the richest materials; they go nowhere on foot but always in sedans, on horseback, or in boats and with numerous attendents following them. With a few honorable exceptions, all the missionaries live in this manner; and thus, as they never mix with people, they make but few converts.      Father Matteo Ripa*

John Thomson: Shen kuei-fen, Tung Hsün and Mao Ch'ang-hsi, Chinese ministers of the Grand Council, c1868. Tung Hsün was a leader of the modernization movement of the 1860's and did much to revitalize an intellectual interest in the West.

98    Photographer unknown: Early Chinese railroad, c1880.

Photographer unknown: Plague inspectors, Hong Kong, c1890. The plague that broke out in the
1890's in T'ai-p'ing Shan, the western district of Hong Kong, continued sporadically until the 1920's.

100      Photographer unknown: U.S.S. *Monocacy* laid up during the winter in North China, c1870.

Underwood and Underwood: Bengal Lancers escorting Alfred von Waldersee, Supreme Commander of the Allied Forces, to Meridian Gate, entrance to Forbidden City, Peking, 1900. Count von Waldersee directed the final operations after the Boxer Uprising.

102    Thomas Childe: Gate in Peking wall, c1880.

Donald Mennie: Wan-hsien, Yangtze River, c1925.

Attributed to John Thomson: Transportation by wheelbarrow, c1865. A farmer and pig share a ride to market on a Chinese-style wheelbarrow, a common form of conveyance in much of central and northern China. Pigs were often given alcohol to keep them from struggling.

Joseph F. Rock: Villagers listening to a phonograph, Ch'ing-shui, eastern Kansu, April 11, 1925.

106    Photographer unknown: "Mugging" for the camera, c1875.

Photographer unknown: Chinese family, c1875.

John Thomson: Manchu brides, c1868. Ideally, a bride was expected to be amiable, of few words, industrious and moderately good-looking.

Photographer unknown: Manchu women, c1875.

Thomas Childe: Cityscape, c1877.

Photographer unknown: Pagoda in Ningpo, c1865. Ningpo was one of the
five ports opened to the West as a result of the Treaty of Nanking (1842).

H. C. White (?): Thousand Colonnade Promenade, New Summer Palace, c1925.

*Five p.m. — I have just returned from the Summer Palace. It is really a fine thing, like an English park — numberless buildings with handsome rooms, and filled with Chinese curios, and handsome clocks, bronzes, etc. But, alas! such a scene of desolation. The French General [de Montauban, jointly in command of the allied forces with General Grant] came up full of protestations. He had prevented looting in order that all the plunder might be divided between the armies, etc., etc. There was not a room that I saw in which half the things had not been taken away or broken to pieces. I tried to get a regiment of ours sent to guard the place, and then sell the things by auction, but it is difficult to get things done by system in such a case, so some officers are left who are to fill two or three carts with treasures which are to be sold. . . . Plundering and devastating a place like this is bad enough, but what is much worse is the waste and breakage. . . . French soldiers were destroying in every way the most beautiful silks, breaking the jade ornaments and porcelain, etc. War is a hateful business. The more one sees of it the more one detests it.*    Lord Elgin

*With regard to the destruction of the summer palace, I believe that, politically speaking, it was a mistake. It was necessary that some great reprisal should be made for the outrages committed by the Chinese; but the destruction should have taken place inside the city, and not twelve miles off; for so ignorant are . . . the Chinese of what passes outside their four walls, that there are many here in Peking who . . . believe that we had to pay an indemnity for leave to withdraw our troops, and that we are here on sufferance. . . . In the provinces people must be still further from the truth. . . . Had the Imperial Palace in Peking been destroyed the matter would have been notorious to all, and its recollection would not have been blown away with the last cloud of smoke from the Yuen-Ming-Yuen [Summer Palace].*    A. S. F. Mitford

*There was music. . . . All had spread out their cloths and knelt and prostrated themselves, before a priest took up his position standing behind each, and extended both hands to hold the novice's head quite steady, fingers widespread, so as especially to shield the eyes, all of course closed. . . . There were sixty-eight young men and women, all kneeling with their eyes closed, their faces turned up to heaven, and with nine little charcoal cones smouldering on each of their bare pates . . . whilst they prayed one and all, as it seemed with their hearts. . . . My place was by the nuns, and one moved, so that one of the smouldering cones fell off and into her bosom; and another did not cry out, but roared — roared like a child. . . . Meanwhile, the cones smouldered down till they just charred those marks with which we are familiar on priests' heads; then they went out, though all that day and on into the next, several little unburnt lumps were still adhering to the poor consecrated heads.     Mrs. Archibald Little*

*(Canton, Dec. 20th, 1898) We were shown three temples — the Doctors Temple, the Temple of the 500 Genii and the Chun Ancestor Temple. The Doctor seemed popular . . . built in memory of a famous physician, the people have made a splendid pile wherin to worship the Doctor and pray for his healing power. In the next room you pray for good luck and the little gods seated in a circle give you answer through the curved sticks, an improved method of flipping a penny. You can't help wondering what kind of a chap this Doctor was.*

*The 500 Genii are 500 gilded statues of the sitting . . . all variously ugly!     Eliphalet Huntington Blatchford*

John Thomson: Pagoda Island, ten miles below Foochow, at mouth of Min River, c1868.

Felice A. Beato: Hall of Prayer for Harvests, at Temple of Heaven, Peking, c1860. The emperor made periodic
visits to the monument in order to communicate with Heaven, the only superior force he recognized.

John Thomson: "Altar of Heaven," Foochow, near Min River, c1868.

Photographer unknown: Buddhist monks, 1873. Posed in a photographer's studio,
118  four monks hold articles commonly associated with the practice of Buddhism.

John Thomson: Temple at Yen-p'ing, Fukien, c1868.

120     Philip H. Egerton: Kee Monastery, near southwestern Chinese border, 1863.

Photographer unknown: Ming tombs, Nanking, c1865. Before the capital was moved to Peking in 1421, the first three Ming
emperors were buried in Nanking. The paths to the main tomb are guarded by statues of military warriors and civilian officials.

John Henry Hinton: Bamboo grove, Mohkansan region near Soochow Creek, 1910.

John Thomson: On the Min River, c1868.

*Nowhere so vividly as in China does one realise that not only the path of glory but every other kind of path leads but to a grave. . . . The omega-shaped tombs of south China are apt . . . to appal one by their vastness and too often by the barren cheerlessness of their surroundings. But there is nothing dismal in the family graveyards that dot the . . . country districts in the north. . . . We find only little hillocks and unpretentious gravestones.     R. F. Johnston*

*The family must be there when anyone dies. I made the little red bag which was to provide her with comforts for the journey and hung it on her button hole. I cut a piece of silver from an earring that she might have silver to buy what she needed, and put it in the bag with a pinch of tea and a piece of candy and a bit of salt vegetable to make her food more palatable. And, according to custom, as my old aunt died, as the breath left her body, I stuffed the little red bag into her mouth that she might have food to eat on her journey. I placed in her hand the small bundle of food which she needed to feed the dogs as she crossed the great Dog Mountain. I bound her feet together so that her body should not get up again. I did all the things for her that a son or a daughter-in-law or a daughter should do.     Ning Lao T'ai-t'ai*

*Over the bend of the arbor, there are a few lean hard*
*Branches of elms that have not quite caught up with spring.*
*They are now imprinted in a sky of fish scales*
*Like a page of light blue clouded writing paper*
*On which monk Huai-ssu has scribbled his*
*Cursive script of iron and silver strokes.     Wen I-to*

Photographer unknown: On the road to Ku-shan, western China, c1860.

125

# Westerners in China

Of all lands, China was for Westerners the most mysterious, the most frequently the subject of wonder, of speculation, of tales of magic and monsters. From far back, the West marveled at what the Greeks called the "Seres," or Silk People. Rome, about the time of Christ, passed laws limiting silk importation in order to stem the alarming flow of gold from its coffers to the fabled, shimmering land in the East that produced such miraculous material and remained itself so completely unknown.

While a land route across Asia had been used for untold centuries by intermediaries who carried items of trade between Europe and China, European use of a sea route to China was pioneered by the Portuguese only in the early sixteenth century. From that time on, Sino-Western contact and confrontation became something to reckon with. Not, however, until the late decades of the eighteenth century did the juxtaposition of the two areas in the persons of various Western traders, priests and others become a matter of real concern to either side.

But even then it was the West that desired increased and closer contacts. China, convinced of her cultural superiority, failed to perceive that the Westerners on her shores were harbingers of a new era. By 1842 British demands for additional trading rights and the Chinese attempt to stop the inward flow of opium resulted in a lost war for China. Foreign invasion coincided with the decline of the dynasty's ability to govern; the classic problem for China's empire—the simultaneous appearance of strong barbarians on the borders and domestic turmoil—suggested to growing numbers of Chinese that the Mandate of Heaven was soon to be taken from the alien Manchu dynasty. Thus the first cameras to enter China would record glimpses of what was in many respects a troubled land.

---

Any person arriving on the shores of China from the West in the mid-1800's was almost certain to be male and either a trader or a missionary. To be sure, there were a few wanderers and eccentrics who were neither of these (although the Victorian adjective "intrepid" is certainly the most fitting description for any such voyagers), a handful of whom had acquired an addiction to the new invention of photography. It is to their efforts that we owe at least the early images in this volume.

Two aspects are especially noteworthy in considering China and the West, Chinese and Westerners, in the middle and later decades of the last

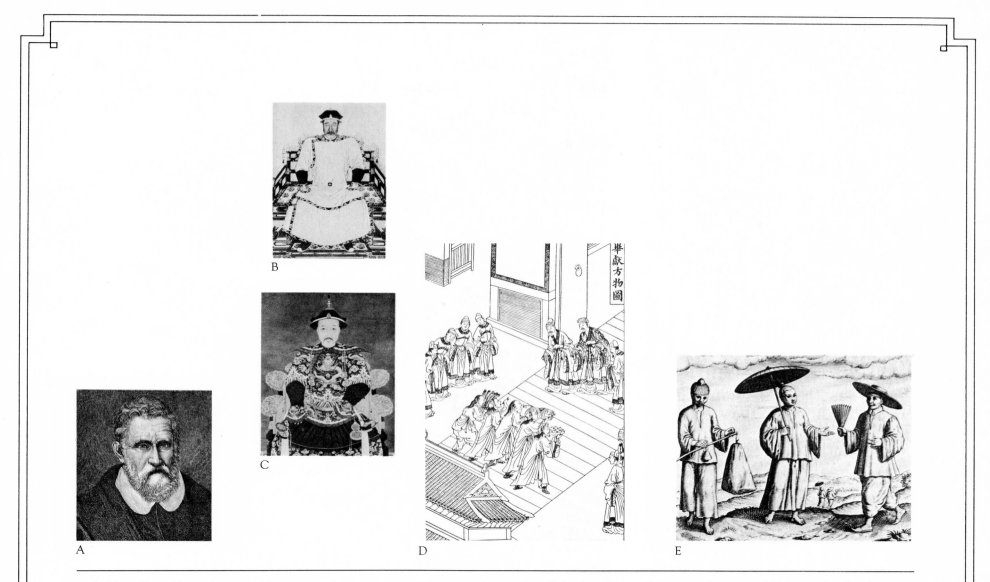

A. Marco Polo, thirteenth-century Venetian merchant spent seventeen years in China as an official under the Mongols. He was the first European to write about everyday China, though much of what he reported met with disbelief.
B. Nurhachi (1559–1626) unified the Manchu tribes in the northeast. When the Ming dynasty fell to a rebel, Nurhachi's descendants established the Ch'ing ("Pure") dynasty in Peking (1644).
C. Emperor Kung-tsi (r. 1662–1722), whose long reign achieved the consolida-

tion of Manchu rule over China, actively supported Chinese cultural endeavors and at the same time showed interest in Western science.
D. Paying homage to the emperor of China and ultimately establishing grounds for trade, barbarians present gifts of tribute to Peking officials.
E. Trading in Bantam, a Dutch settlement in the East Indies, these sixteenth-century "overseas" Chinese merchants came in contact with traders from Europe who sought pepper and spices from the Orient.

century. The first is the outstanding sense of adventure implicit in embarking for China, either from Europe or from the Americas; the second, the outstanding ignorance of the Western voyagers to China about the land and the people they were setting out to reach. Whether in the service of their own curiosity, or their God, or in search of fortune in new lands, few had the slightest idea of the quality, the reality, far less the roots of the civilization awaiting them at journey's end.

Men had been sailing to China for many centuries before the nineteenth even dawned. Arab traders hugged the coast of East Africa, rounded the great triangle of India, sailed through the scattered islands of the Burma coast, down the straits between Malaysia and the vast mysterious tangle of Sumatran jungles, past the muddy little island swamp that was to become Singapore, all the way up to Thailand and finally through the little archipelago that includes Hong Kong Island and surrounds the Pearl River delta in South China. No one really knows when these first mariners with their dark and, to the Chinese, exaggerated features arrived, but a sage estimate would place the date at least 2,000 years ago. When the Arabs learned how to use the monsoon winds blowing in contrary directions at different times of the year (the word "monsoon" derives from an Arab word for "season"), trade slowly increased manufactures of many kinds. And, like all commerce, it was accompanied by the exchange of ideas and techniques.

By the early T'ang dynasty in China (A.D. 618–906), the capital Ch'ang-an, near modern Sian, was unquestionably the most cosmopolitan city in the world. Probably few of its foreign population had come by sea, however, for the overland route—the long trail over Central Asian wastes, romantically named "Silk Road," whose camel-borne trade so depleted the coffers of Rome and was subsequently to bring Chinese porcelains to the Near East—was available and heavily traveled.

There were foreigners not only in the capital, but in firmly established settlements round the southern coastal regions. And foreign religions— Buddhism, entering from India in the first century A.D., the heretical Nestorian form of Christianity from Syria, Manichaeism, Zoroastrianism and later Islam itself—flourished in parts of Chinese realms and had their Chinese adherents. It was not until later in the same T'ang dynasty that the Chinese equivalent of the English "dissolution of the monasteries" would undertake to erase all except Buddhism from the life of China. Wu Tsung, the emperor under whose decree this cleansing was attempted, made a statement which is central to understanding China and its people at this and later times. He declared, in A.D. 845, his determination to "dry up this vile source of errors which flood the empire . . . so that in the customs of our people there shall be no mixture."

This xenophobic attitude, with its implicit opinion that the civilization of China was the sole significant one on earth, was in the T'ang probably more official than popular. But in time, with a century of later Mongol occupation and rule, it was to become an ingrained general conviction of all Chinese who pondered the question or encountered a Westerner. The parallelism in world overview between the West and China is striking, even if in each hemisphere the causes were not entirely similar. By the Ming dynasty (1368–1644), when the first Western seafarers arrived, and with increased emphasis in the nineteenth century, when the habits of the West in China were clear to all, the collisions of the two attitudes grew in importance and gravity. The blind conviction on both sides of innate superiority, less understandable in the Westerners because they at least had the chance to study the other civilization in its home and at first hand, was bound to lead to tragedy. As in many a confrontation, pride led to violence, to buttressed pride and to further violence.

In the time of Mongol rule in China (1279–1368)—a painful century inadequately understood and only partially chronicled by Marco Polo, who, like nineteenth-century photographers, saw only what he thought he understood—it was again true that the capital, now at Peking, was a cosmopolitan place. By now the trade routes over Asia were flourishing, and maritime trade continued fast. There was a Catholic archbishop in Peking, and various other Christians came and went, making a few converts and building scattered churches.

With the expulsion of the hated Mongols, Christianity seems to have vanished, too, as did Westerners except on rare trading visits. The great Ming dynasty was taking no chances of another barbarian invasion. Its scholars and statesmen stressed the necessity of a return to Chinese orthodoxy and to the self-sufficiency of the empire. It was not until more than 200 years later, in the decline of the Ming dynasty when the degenerate ruling house showed unmistakable signs of losing its grip on the Mandate of Heaven (a term meaning the right to rule and dating from Confucius, nearly five centuries before Christ), that a clutch of Western Christians reached Peking. One of them, Matteo Ricci, a Jesuit priest who established a residence there in 1601, was perhaps the greatest European ever to live and work in China.

In the late Ming, and in the ensuing Ch'ing dynasty (1644–1912), when China was again ruled by a non-Chinese people, tribal Manchus who broke through the physical and cultural barrier of the Great Wall, Ricci and his missionary successors had little success. Ricci's original opinion that only by penetrating the ranks of the scholar-bureaucracy itself, and reaching the emperor and the court, would Christianity have any chance of success in China proved correct, though success in this case meant hardly more than the gaining of limited tolerance. The Ch'ing emperors and courtiers found that the scientific skills of the Jesuits in astronomy, mathematics, painting in the Western manner, engineering and cartography could be important aids in various government affairs ranging from mapping the whole of China to casting cannon for use in frontier wars to painting the emperors' horses. They discovered new playthings—chiming clocks with moving marionette figures, steam-jet–propelled boats for sailing on the imperial lakes, the telescope—which might be thrown away when they became tiresome. In fact, the Chinese themselves were the first to conceive of the escapement mechanism essential to clockwork, and their mapmaking prowess was far superior to that of the West by the turn of the tenth century, but science did not interest Confucian scholars and China's scientific achievements were downplayed by them, largely unknown to others.

Christianity got lost amid the practical business of cartography and winding the hundreds of clocks in the palaces. But when it raised its head and made itself conspicuous, the results were an upsurge of Chinese anti-Christian feeling and persecution of both priests and converts. In the time of Emperor K'ang-hsi (r. 1662-1722), the greatest of all Manchu rulers and one with some claim to rank among the greatest of Chinese occupants of the Dragon Throne, the Rites Controversy erupted at court. The Jesuits, whether for diplomatic or other reasons, had always held that Chinese reverence for their ancestors, which is central to Confucian orthodoxy, was secular and not religious. This was hotly disputed by others, particularly the Dominicans in China,

A. As Western influence increased, the church became a familiar sight in China. The perpendicular spires, erected without approval from a geomancer, offended the Chinease peasantry and were believed to interrupt the spirits' course of travel.

B. A Chinese colporteur offers a Bible to a Cantonese. Books were considered precious acquisitions, and the Bible spread rapidly throughout China.

C. Matteo Ricci (1552~1610), Italian Jesuit priest (left), outraged Chinese officials and scholars when he constructed a world map placing China off-center. (right) Paul Hsu, Ricci's prize convert.

D. (top) An anti-Christian cartoon depicts missionaries extracting eyes for use in alchemy. (bottom) Thanks to a play on words in Chinese, the hog represents the Christian god. *Yeh-su* (the characters on the animal's body) is the transliteration of "Jesus."

and eventually the Pope sent to Peking one of the most unbending and polemical papal legates on record, Cardinal de Tournon. Against the advice and pleas of the Christian community there, this rash man proceeded to tell the emperor (who was kindly disposed to his team of Jesuit priests at court) that ancestor worship was heretical for a Christian, and that no Chinese could be a Christian if he persisted in the practice. K'ang-hsi was greatly annoyed, and many Christians in China realized that the Cardinal's actions had threatened their cause. The Cardinal was convinced that he had done the only right thing; he retired south to Macao, where he died of a fever.

It was during the following reign that Christians were either expelled or persecuted in numbers. The reason given was simply that of Wu Tsung in the T'ang dynasty: to expunge the foreign evil from the purity of Chinese Confucian life. The same reason was to be given again in the nineteenth century, when the pseudo-Christian Taiping rebels were put down with difficulty.

The point that must be made is twofold. The Manchus had become in all significant ways as Chinese as the Chinese themselves, and the ancient form of Confucian state bureaucracy was upheld by them as fiercely as ever it was by the Chinese. For 2,000 years and more, Confucian teachings had been codified not as a religion but as a set of universally accepted rules by which society was regulated. The key was respect for everyone in a higher position: sons for father and elder relatives, including elder brothers; daughters for parents and also for brothers whether elder or not; and so on, in terms of lineage, class, position, upward in an ever-narrowing pyramid until the great ministers of state were to be found knocking their heads on the ground in the ritual kowtow before the emperor. The emperor himself kowtowed before Heaven, the sole master he acknowledged and with which he acted as intermediary on behalf of all mankind. Conversely, authority passed down the pyramid from apex to base.

Even the brilliant Ricci did not fully realize the implications of Christianity to the Chinese. Later, several learned priests in the early Ch'ing decades probably did, but hoped to get by in demonstrating the scientific superiority of the West—a superiority which was, had they but known it, a very recent development. They were convinced that the triumph of science in high Chinese circles would eventually bring in its train the realization that Christianity was the mainspring of these achievements. In fact, the Chinese genius in science, now being revealed in the lifework of Western scientific historian Dr. Joseph Needham, was never really incorporated into Confucian thought. Science, to the Chinese, was a matter more appropriate for a pastime than for the serious consideration of scholar-bureaucrats. Painting and literature, especially the Classics (a curious echo of the Western reverence for the dead-language masterpieces in Latin and Greek until well into the twentieth century), were considered the heights of Chinese genius—and truly they were, together with porcelain of such virtuosity that it still astounds. But no other branch of man's achievements outside the accepted Confucian concerns was fit to be included.

Against this wall the West was to batter its head in several ways, but always with the same negative effect. In the end it was not a Western religion that finally began to open China to Europeans and Americans during the nineteenth century, but determined traders backed by the guns of their governments.

The Portuguese reached China first (ironically with the aid of a Chinese invention, the compass), knocking forcibly on the doors of that seemingly

131

hermetic civilization with cannon powered by gunpowder (another Chinese invention). They had at that time two *idées fixes*: the absolute right to trade with whomsoever they wanted and the necessity of converting to the Catholic faith all "pagans" encountered in their dealings. Historian C. P. Fitzgerald puts the matter succinctly: "The early Western visitors were of a character which confirmed the Chinese view of them as 'barbarians' . . . . Only the hope of great profit and the courage of reckless adventurers could induce men to undertake voyages [to China] on which the prospect of safe return was at best fifty-fifty. It was, consequently, not the most learned, cultivated, mature element in Western civilization which the Chinese first encountered. . . ."

Since the Portuguese were followed by other nations who in varying degrees repeated the same pattern, subsequent learned missionary personnel were hard-put to convince the Chinese that they were anything but, at best, more enlightened examples of the "barbarous" races to which they belonged. The continuing acts and attitudes of mercantile Westerners, and even of some missionaries, did not redress the balance. They merely substantiated Chinese opinion. This is part of the background against which

all Western nineteenth- and early twentieth-century reactions to China must be seen.

One of the most curious elements —and, it would turn out, one of the saddest—in the story of contacts between the West and China is that the written experiences of all those hundreds, even thousands of Westerners which were and are on record in the West appear largely to have escaped the attention of later travelers to China, era after era. Thus each new wave of men (and later, women) from the West tended to have no more knowledge of China and its people than did the first Nestorian Christians, the first Jesuits, the first Portuguese and other traders, and so on.

The first Portuguese, who in any case despised as "Moors" all peoples outside the boundaries of Europe, came to China in a state of crude ignorance. Ricci and his confrères appear never to have heard of the letters of the first archbishop of Peking, or of the tales of Marco Polo (then in numerous copies in Rome and elsewhere). The surprising, later shocking fact is that there was no accumulated body of information on China readily available to those about to set out for what was romantically called "Cathay" (a name characteristically

derived not from that of a Chinese dynasty but from the Khitans, a group of tribal conquerors of part of China at an earlier date). Even by the beginning of the twentieth century, despite some remarkable exceptions, there was meager serious study done on the most populous, longest-lived empire the world has known. The lending libraries so popular in Europe and America of that time contained little else but romantic and uncomprehending narratives by stray travelers who with rather gushing sentiments penned those appalling Victorian travelogues. Only within the austere confines of various academic libraries were translations of Confucian books available—one of the keys to understanding China. Among the works most frequently read were books by missionaries whose comprehension of the springs of Chinese civilization was in most cases rudimentary. Like the Chinese, who opined that what was not Chinese was "barbarian," the missionaries were inclined to think that all that was Chinese was simply "pagan" and could be dismissed as a terrible reflection of a people without the benefits of Christian faith.

The situation was made dangerous by the fact that in the decades following the Opium War (1839–42), since missionaries were protected by the clauses in treaties with their own governments specifying "extraterritoriality" (the right of all foreigners to immunity from Chinese laws and to judgment by their own), they tended to hold an umbrella of immunity over their "converts"—to the disgust and futile rage of others. An extract from a confidential report of a six-month journey in 1897 through northeast China made by Colonel Browne, Military Attaché at the British Legation in Peking, introduces this point and brings out its repercussions:

"It is, perhaps, not strange in this country that though the foreigner is despised, the native who follows the creed of the foreigner frequently obtains power and influence to which he could not otherwise attain. The reason for this is that the mass of the upper classes regard the missionaries as political agents and fear them. The poor know this, and look, in many cases, to the missionary—the honest for protection, the dishonest to further their own ends. These ends may be the evasion of the recovery of a debt, or some similar dispute, in which they know that their connection with the Church will influence the Magistrate. It *ought not* to do so, for the Presbyterian Missionaries lose no opportunity of letting the Magistrates and others know that they will use no influence when a Christian is before the Court, whether as complainant or defendant; but practically, it *does* influence them, for they attach the same value to these statements by the missionaries as they would to a declaration made by themselves in similar circumstances. . . . Roman Catholic priests are simple-minded, hard-working men with no ambition beyond the success of the work to which they have devoted their lives, but they are under a Bishop who directs their policy, and the policy is such as to give ground for the opinion held by many Chinese that missionaries are sent to this land in the interests of their own Government.

"The Bishop's passport is said to be technically worded so that he appears to be appointed by the French Government: he travels with a retinue, and flies the French flag in Mukden, and in any town in which he is temporarily residing. Every case in which a convert is concerned is taken up as a case against the Church: it is therefore no surprise that their members are said to be more numerous than those of the Presbyterian Church."

The Ch'ing government, having acceded to the foreign powers' treaties at gunpoint, were in the terminal dilemma of being unable to deal fairly with their own subjects for fear of breaking a treaty provision, or at least of offending a foreign nation. Thus the government, alternately propped up and chastised by foreign powers, often appeared in its latter decades to be a mere tool in their hands, the welfare of its subjects no longer within its grasp.

The inability to take seriously either the people or the institutions of the country in which they lived and worked, as missionaries, merchants or diplomats, could only lead in the short and long run to deep antagonisms.

The Chinese themselves, even the most highly educated, were deeply ignorant of the West. They had rarely gone beyond the states on China's periphery, with which they traded and dominated as tributaries, and they certainly never attempted to dominate the rest of the globe and its peoples, so there was some excuse for their attitude toward foreigners. Regarded in varying degrees as "barbarians," in itself a reflection of China's historical contacts with neighbors, this concept was woven into orthodox opinion. The word *i* referred to all non-Chinese, whether from the settled or the nomadic tribes of Asia, the South Seas or the West. One treaty between Britain and China, signed at gunpoint as usual, contained a clause forbidding the use of the character *i* in all Chinese official correspondence.

Reading through the many hun-

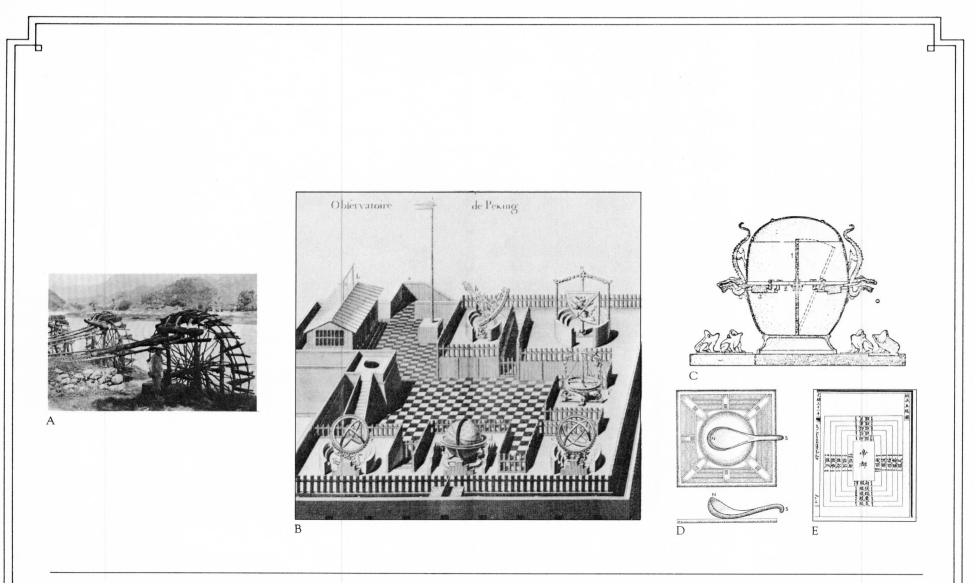

A. The Chinese developed an elaborate water technology. Despite rough land and rocky terrain, these irrigation wheels, propelled by the river current, raise the water level as much as forty feet.

B. Jesuit illustration of the Peking Observatory. The emperor maintained his connection with Heaven by devising the Lunar Calendar, dating seasonal changes and predicting eclipses. Since astrological events were important to Chinese governing power, seventeenth-century Jesuits were esteemed for their more accurate astronomical devices and knowledge of trigonometrics.

C. Cross-section of Chang Heng's seismograph (eight Han feet high). The tipping of the pendulum and the trajectory of the ball from the dragon's mouth to that of a frog indicated the direction of the earth's tremor.

D. The lodestone-filled spoon of this early compass responded to magnetic forces by rotating on its dish. The Chinese perfected the first modern compass by A.D. 1100.

F. An idealized traditional Chinese view of the world. Radiating from the center, "City of the Emperor," zones represent decreasing degrees of civilization: feudal lordship to barbarianism to total savagery.

dreds of thousands of letters from missionaries in China, or sampling that veritable deluge of general works about the country, the inescapable impression is of an uncivilized people (although occasionally a measure of civilization is accorded to members of the bureaucracy). Yet it is a fact that until little over a century before the nineteenth the Chinese were, in scientific discovery and applied science, at least the equals of if not superior to the Western nations. In terms of philosophical inquiry and in the construction of systematic philosophies of great penetration, in terms of literature and art, the Chinese had nothing to fear from Western equivalents. They had invented, in some cases more than a thousand years before Europeans, watertight compartments in ships and several other key nautical engineering designs, deep drilling (for brine, not oil), the rotary winnowing machine, the wheelbarrow, and various hydraulic devices.

Disinterested China made little attempt to discover the world, and if possible took even less trouble to understand the national systems of other countries until the need to survive their attacks was thrust on her in the nineteenth century. There is no history of Chinese overseas adventures beyond East and Southeast Asia apart from a brief, unique period in the early Ming when ships went as far as East Africa on voyages of discovery. Even the abortive invasions of Japan were Mongol, not Chinese.

China maintained her traditional frontiers by employing a system of tribute. States or groups of peoples on or near her borders were invited to send regular tributary missions to the capital—often twice a year—and there such parties were met, escorted, properly housed and fed at Chinese expense. The gifts they brought for the emperor were counted and receipted by a special department of the central government, then placed in store. Discussions were held at various levels between the tributary party and officials designated to deal with affairs in the tributary states. In this way, the Chinese kept abreast of foreign affairs that actually or potentially involved their own interests on the frontiers and beyond. Political groupings and military movements were noted and could be countered in various ways, generally by political maneuvering, when necessary by punitive armed force. Finally, after making their kowtows at an imperial audience, the tribute bearers were sent on their way, loaded with gifts usually much more valuable than the exotica they had brought—having had in the meanwhile ample opportunity to trade with Chinese merchants.

The idea of colonies was not an integral part of Chinese thought. Such colonies of Chinese as did exist from at least T'ang times on the shores and river mouths of Southeast Asian countries were in the nature of resident trader facilities which distributed Chinese products and collected local goods for the return voyages. The various characteristic spices of the Nan Yang (the South Seas, but meaning the archipelagos of the region), the cobalt for the blue of blue-and-white porcelain decoration (called "Sumatran blue" because it was transshipped there on arrival from the Middle East), the hornbill ivory (the frontal boss and beak of the Indonesian *kenyalang* bird) which was in demand for delicate carvings—such materials as these were the usual imports, often carried in non-Chinese ships.

The seaward frontier was ridden with pirates, to a greater or lesser extent at different times, and China dealt with this problem piecemeal and pragmatically. For a land with such an immense coastline, it may seem surprising that China did not develop naval strength during the Ch'ing period, but it is no wonder that the nineteenth-century maritime incursions by the West were slow to arouse any Chinese reaction in naval terms. A glance at a map shows that China would hardly need to acquire naval strength for defense before then. The nearest large land masses are Taiwan with its (then) tribal population, developing as a serious piratical threat only under the encouragement of the seventeenth-century Dutch, and Korea, which was long tributary to China. Though during the Ming dynasty Japanese pirates had periodically pillaged China's rich southeastern coastal regions, during the Ch'ing period Japan lived in a relative isolation of its own until Commodore Perry arrived in the 1850's; only after that did Japan develop a modern naval power. Even the bloodthirsty Portuguese, in their carracks bristling with guns, eventually settled for the little peninsula of Macao on the estuary of the Pearl River leading to Canton. And the Spaniards had enough on their hands while trying to control the congeries of Philippine tribes. How could they toy with an invasion of China?

In the last decade of the eighteenth century the prelude to Western intervention in China was played as the British government sent an embassy headed by one of the most cultured men of his times, Lord Macartney, to see the emperor of China and to deal with what was viewed as the unsatisfactory state of trade and intercourse between the two countries. The Chinese found it easy to sell shiploads of tea, porcelains, craft products, silk and, curiously, rhubarb to British merchants. But the primary item that Britain found salable at Canton—the one port where they were permitted to trade, for six months of the year—was opium, the importation of which was forbidden. Thus ways and means had to be found to introduce it. Local authorities up and down the coast as well as at Canton were bribed, and a spy network (on some occasions involving missionaries) operated to ensure a flow of information on suitable times and places for landing the contraband. Most opium was grown under duress by the British East India Company in India, where it was sold to private traders who carried it to China for great profits. The Chinese paid for it in silver, and that metal now flowed increasingly into Western treasuries.

Macartney, however, did not go to Peking with his valuable gifts to talk about opium. The subject was never mentioned on either side. He was to try to establish diplomatic relations on the usual basis by an exchange of ambassadors and to negotiate a less restricting basis for trade.

The courtesy and generosity of his reception were matched only by the absoluteness of the negatives he received in answer to his diplomatically expressed requests. He was royally entertained, but his questions were adroitly sidestepped by the Chinese. Eventually, he was assured that the winter of North China was severe and that his party could hardly be expected to survive it with comfort. His return down the Grand Canal, with a load of munificent Chinese gifts, was one he and his party found intensely interesting and exciting, but in his dispatch box he carried letters from Emperor Ch'ien-lung (r. 1736–95) addressed to George III of Britain. These are now classics in the history of diplomatic correspondence:

"You, O King, live beyond the confines of many seas; nevertheless, impelled by your humble desire to partake of the benefits of our civilization, you have dispatched a mission respectfully bearing your memorial. Your Envoy crossed the seas and paid his respects at my Court on the anniversary of my birthday. To show your devotion you have also sent offerings of your country's produce. . . .

"As to what you have requested in your message, O King, namely to be allowed to send one of your subjects to reside in the Celestial Empire and to look after your Country's trade, this does not conform to the Celestial Empire's ceremonial system and defi-

A. The Earl of Macartney was sent by Britain to the court of Ch'ien-lung to secure better trade facilities in China, as well as a formal diplomatic relationship. He was politely turned away. European desire for increased trade and diplomatic equality eventually led to the Opium Wars of 1839-42 and 1856-60.

B. The procession of Emperor Ch'ien-lung, in his palanquin, is approached by the Earl of Macartney.

C. Opium den, Canton. The smoking of opium, once used only for medicinal purposes, became a hazardous pastime. By 1890 perhaps 10 percent of the Chinese population were addicted to the drug, which they called "foreign mud."

D. Attack and capture of Chuenpi (c1840): a romanticized view of well-organized British troops.

E. Robert Cornelius Napier of Magdala (b. Ceylon, 1810), British field marshal. In 1860, under Sir Hope Grant, Napier stormed and dismantled the forts north of the Pei-ho and advanced to Peking, where the Chinese surrendered at the end of the Second Opium War.

F. Lord Elgin, signer of the treaties of Tientsin and Peking, Second Opium War.

nitely cannot be done. . . . The Celestial Empire, ruling all within the four seas . . . does not value ingenious articles, nor do we have the slightest need of your Country's manufactures."

Although all that Ch'ien-lung wrote to Britain's king was unquestionably accurate in relation to China's perceived needs, and to her superiority in power over all contiguous or near neighbors by land and by sea, what was not factual and had not been so for at least a century was that China was the greatest power in the world.

It is probable that the emperor and court—indeed, Chinese officialdom and the scholar elite as a whole—were unable to realize this, and that Ch'ien-lung's words were sincere enough. To a society that had never had any permanent use for "manufactures" of ingenuity and foreign provenance, even those given by the British ambassador in hundreds and ranging from a hot-air balloon to scientific instruments and an orrery, there was no occasion for a change of heart. It was a change of head that was required in China.

Lord Macartney summed up his opinions of China and the Chinese government in terms of Western ideas of the inevitability of progress. Even he proved no better in the end at understanding the real mainsprings of Chinese life and thought than others

of his and later times. ". . . it would now seem," he wrote, "that the policy of the Court . . . concurred in endeavouring to keep out of sight whatever can manifest our British pre-eminence, which they undoubtedly feel. It is, however, vain to attempt arresting the progress of human knowledge. The human mind is of a soaring nature and having once gained the lower steps of the ascent, struggles incessantly against every difficulty to reach the highest." True as this was—and still is—in Western life, the soaring nature of the Chinese mind did not manifest itself in terms comparable to the capitalist expansion of the West, with its natural sequel, the necessity for foreign trade.

The Chinese, through lack of knowledge of the West, and through their disinterest in most of the rest of the world after the conclusion of the great Ming expeditions in the early fifteenth century, did not understand what would happen when their own Confucian system encountered the manifestations of another powerful system. Sufficient for them was the knowledge that their way of thought and government, which for two millenniums had proved easily the most flexible as well as the longest-lived form of society and organization, was still with them. They found it unbelievable that such a

finely tempered and well-tried thing could fail to stem the aggressive acts of the foreigners.

The product of Western philosophies, as Macartney had rightly indicated, was something that the dominant trends of Chinese thought had never pursued—a searching mind that reaches out to inquire with boundless curiosity about everything in the world and attempts the exploration of the world itself. We need not enter the scholarly lists and tilt at reasons why Confucianism tended to be hermetic and to want to stay that way, or why the reverse was true of post-Renaissance European thought. The facts are there, spelled out in the sad results of the collision that took place.

The meaning of historical events is seldom apparent to those most directly involved in them. And so it was in China of the last century. Most Westerners were unable to grasp in any depth the implications of what they saw with their eyes. A dynasty was in rapid decline, but what was much more important to the 400 million Chinese at that time was the dissolution of their ancient system of political thought and action. As the century went on, the demonstration of national bankruptcy in every field was painful, bewildering, humiliating. And even had another dynasty supplanted that of the Manchus when it fell, as the Chinese Ming did the Mongol, it is not likely that it could have done more than make a few feeble gestures of self-defense. Even without the massive interference in China's affairs by Western powers that hastened the end of the Ch'ing, the dynasty would have fallen. We have only to look at the massive Taiping Rebellion of the mid-nineteenth century, suppressed after long struggle and with Western help, to realize the inherent spirit of revolt by that time in the minds of the Chinese.

The scene on which the cameras of professionals and amateurs directed their brass-bound lenses in mid-century China was a sorry one indeed. It was a China in the dotage of a long life, a China in the confusion and turmoil of the recent past and the actual present, shaped by defeat at the hands of the West and by unrest within. Yet, since most Westerners considered these facts to be of less importance than their own right to trade even at the expense of increasing the misery of the Chinese, their attitude usually did not include any real involvement with China or its fate. Most were essentially onlookers, uncaring about China itself and with a deeply vested interest in exploiting the Chinese or their situation for personal or religious reasons.

The sale of opium continued to be increasingly profitable to the British (and, to a lesser extent, the Americans, who obtained supplies from Turkey) so that nothing would persuade them to give it up—neither national honor, which was occasionally invoked in the British parliament, nor the protests of the Chinese, whose economy was being undermined and whose laws were being flouted. By the early decades of the nineteenth century, silver was draining alarmingly from the Chinese national purse. Inevitably, the opium question came to a head. It was no longer possible to hide from the emperor payments of silver in, for example, the year 1838-39 for 40,000 chests of opium, each containing about 60 kilos of the prepared drug.

The emperor took action. The imperial commissioner, Lin, was sent to Canton to try to stop the trade. After fruitless negotiations with the British, and a sensible letter sent to Queen Victoria, Lin had no option but to place all merchants who were at the "factories" in Canton under virtual house arrest, withdrawing their servants and food supplies. He then seized their huge stocks of opium and publicly destroyed them before Western witnesses.

This proved too much for British pride. Lin had acted without fully understanding what retort his actions would bring. A British expeditionary force was called for and sent out. The British community sailed downriver and anchored aboard ship in Hong Kong harbor, ill-supplied with food and worse off for water. Hong Kong at this time was a more or less barren island with a few Chinese fishing villages. In due course naval and military forces of the British routed all Chinese forces sent against them in a series of coastal maneuvers, then forced the successor of the now officially disgraced Lin to sign a convention by which Hong Kong Island was ceded to them in 1841.

These hostilities, often called the First Opium War, came to an end with the signing under duress of the Treaty of Nanking in 1842 (which the Chinese quite rightly call the First Unequal Treaty). The treaty opened up many Chinese ports to British commerce and residence, and consuls at each port were appointed. The cession of Hong Kong was confirmed, and China had to pay $6 million for the opium Lin destroyed and $12 million for the cost of the war that the British had forced upon her, plus another $3 million to cover the debts of certain Chinese merchants. The British Foreign Secretary, Lord Palmerston, voicing what was probably a generally approved opinion in England, said of the treaty that "it will form an epoch in the progress of civilization of the human races." He did not add that it was really a license to coin money, poison the people and cause further disruption in the economy of the Chinese state.

Later, in 1855, Palmerston was to write: "The Time is fast coming when we shall be obliged to strike another blow in China. . . . These half-civilized governments such as those of China, Portugal, and Spanish America all require a Dressing every eight or ten years to keep them in order. . . ." The contrary views that were expressed did not carry the day, and an excuse to fight the Chinese again was readily found—a trifling matter over a British-registered small Chinese boat seized by the Chinese at Canton. Palmerston's "Dressing," in the shape of the Second Opium War, was administered in no uncertain manner. This time the expeditionary forces included strong French contingents. They occupied Canton, then sailed up the China coast to the mouth of the Peiho (the river leading toward Peking), extracting, again at gunpoint, the Treaty of Tientsin, another unequal treaty. This treaty consisted of a list of provisions for further commercial domination of the Chinese economy by the West, including the opening of the

Chinese heartland by permitting foreign commerce along the Yangtze River. The importation of opium was expressly permitted, foreigners were allowed immunity from Chinese law, a further vast sum in reparations from China was demanded.

It was the nonratification of this treaty by China that led, two years later in 1860, to the British and French capture of Peking and to the sacking of the imperial Summer Palace. Yet, even a century later, two pious American writers could go on record with: "Opium was not the real *cause*, but only the occasion of the war. The true cause lay in the conceited arrogance of the Chinese government, its utter contempt for treaty obligations entered into, the outrageous restrictions placed upon commerce, and the insulting and intolerable treatment of foreigners." This from a book called *The Progress of World-Wide Missions*, published in 1960.

Thereafter, flocks of eager traders, earnest missionaries of a bewildering number of sects (which greatly confused the Chinese on the subject of Christianity), adventurers of every kind, and, of course, the ardent and intrepid photographers all rushed to China. From 1860 the consolidation of Western power in China and the semicolonial status of China went on apace. The situation of China vis-à-vis

the West was not fundamentally to alter until the success of the Communist revolution in 1949.

It was a disintegrating China and a lordly Western presence that, for the most part, the photographers recorded. By 1860, the Taiping Rebellion had already raged for a decade, cutting a broad swathe as it moved from the south to central China, where it established a rebel capital at Nanking in 1853. By the end of the decade, much of its first attraction and power had evaporated, and a beleaguered rebel stronghold finally succumbed to imperial forces. The rebellion had been a popular one, its forces joined on their apparently unstoppable forward march by peasants all along its path. Karl Marx, in January 31, 1850, wrote: "It is to be rejoiced at that the most ancient and stable empire in the world . . . is on the eve of a social upheaval which, in any case, must have extremely important results for civilization." After the Taiping Rebellion, China could never be the same. Chinese forces, reorganized into provincial armies and supplied with Western arms, finally succeeded in suppressing the rebellion at a loss of an estimated 15 to 20 million lives. These armies were lent assistance inland from Shanghai by the American and

British mercenaries Frederick Townsend Ward (from Salem, Massachusetts) and "Chinese" Gordon, later to become known as "Gordon of Khartoum," backed by Shanghai merchants who saw their fortunes endangered. With the greatest difficulty, the Ch'ing dynasty was propped up on the throne by the dedicated scholar-bureaucrats who saw the foundations of their power crumbling. They and the Westerners in China, who also worried over their insecure position, naturally characterized the rebellion as the work of a misguided sect, its tenets derived from a misunderstood and contorted form of Christian doctrine, out to destroy an immemorial and marvelous system. In fact, to that date, the rebellion was the largest popular revolt ever to occur in China.

The activities of English and American mercenaries were hardly conducive to foreign popularity with the people at large. The Taiping leaders themselves were naive in believing at the outset that since they claimed Christianity as their creed, the West would join them in their rebellion against Manchu oppression. A missionary's son, W. H. Medhurst, and the son of Sir John Bowring, governor of Hong Kong, attempted but failed to contact the Heavenly King, as the Taiping leader was styled. Nonetheless, it was their report, whose "justice and accuracy" is "perhaps open to some question" (according, at least, to one historian of the rebellion), that helped seal the fate of the rebellion as far as Western recognition was concerned.

The rebellion, hopeless failure that it turned out to be, formed a model for Sun Yat-sen in 1911 and the Communists, for the Taiping were the first to conclude that China's continued existence could be achieved by no other means than revolution.

"I am afraid that we are tinkering with a cracked kettle," remarked Sir Robert Hart, an Irishman who served for decades as chief of the Chinese Customs Service, to W. A. P. Martin, American missionary and later the first president of Peking Imperial University. "It is not China that is falling to pieces," said Hart at the end of the Sino-Japanese war, "it is the Powers that are pulling her to pieces. . . . Poor China; and yet it will not wake up to the necessity for real reform. They can be hammered and hectored into giving up anything, but no advice—no warning—will rouse them to strengthening their backbone or sharpening their claws."

Martin, author of *A Cycle of Cathay*, also was convinced that the country was on the brink of chaos but that the reason was the "overweening conceit" of the governing classes: "Proud, haughty, bound up in ceremonial, absolutely ignorant of foreign affairs, the least intelligent of her respectable people." His opinion was that the businessmen and bankers made a "splendid contrast" to the scholar-bureaucrats. Just how he (and others) achieved this wildly inaccurate view, when the rapacity of Chinese merchants and bankers was not only apparent to all but encouraged by their Western counterparts, is hard to understand. The American missionary-turned-educator made it clear that he was less interested in Chinese customs and culture than in promoting change, particularly with the injection of American capital in the form of railroads. "The educated Chinaman, who speaks English, becomes a new man," said Martin in conclusion. True, he often did—a servant to the Westerners.

Yet many foreigners were fascinated and captivated by aspects of China and its people that seemed to them worthy of respect—or in some way better or more graceful or more profound than their Western equivalents. Régis-Evariste Huc, better known as Abbé Huc, spent many years in China in the mid-nineteenth century and understood very fully the principles which underlay its civilization. "The idea of the family is the grand principle," he wrote in his book *l'Empire chinois*, published in the 1850's. "It serves as the basis of society. Filial piety . . . continually recommended in the proclamations of Emperors and the speeches of Mandarins, has become the fundamental root of all other virtues." He continues, drawing a detailed picture of the structure of Chinese society at all levels. This remarkable analysis seems to have been disregarded, as was usually the case with solid information on China, by his fellow Westerners.

Still, we find in the literature on China by those who lived there in this and the last century many eulogies on the Chinese. One penetrating analysis comes from a book by an American, George Kates, called *The Years That Were Fat:* "East and West, finally, direct their considerateness . . . the basis of true courtesy, toward quite different things. Privacy, which we value so highly, does not seem to be among Chinese attainables. Unfeigned curiosity, unsuppressed comment, even simple determination to push forward wherever entrance is not specifically forbidden, are universal traits among the lower classes; and although often innocent enough in intent, they never cease to annoy us. . . . On the other hand, our lack of a sense of gradation, for use even in common

speech, our prompt and ready solutions, above all our active execution of them, breaking down personal safeguards and saving assurances that the Chinese have so carefully built up about themselves; all these are to them offensive and even alarming behaviour."

Other voyagers in China found the grandeur of its landscape astounding. "The scenery of the Yangtze Gorges is the grandest I have ever seen," wrote Oliver G. Ready in a book called *Life and Sport in China* (which cheerfully ignores *la condition humaine* there). It "made a greater impression on me than even that of the Rocky Mountains. In my tiny craft, gazing up at the towering cliffs which rise almost perpendicularly for hundreds and sometimes thousands of feet on either side, I could see caves, terraces and strata, which indicate with a marvellous distinctness the different levels of the river, as during untold ages it has eaten its way through solid rock . . . to its present bed." And, predictably, the author is sobered by the implied insignificance of man amid nature: "Along ledges on the beetling cliffs the ubiquitous Chinaman has built his home and planted orange groves, so that far overhead rich clusters of golden fruit lend an effective touch of colour to the beauty and majesty of the scene. . . .

It is a stirring sight to see a big junk forced by wind and manual power against a strong current. The trackers swarm over rocks and mounds . . . like a pack of hounds, singing, laughing, shouting as they go. . . ." One has to translate the inscriptions cut into the rock at San Men Gorge on the Yellow River to discover the intensity of feeling that produces such invocations of the gods for safe passage in the lethal current; and one has to have experienced hard work in a temperature of far over one hundred degrees Fahrenheit, which is usual in central China in summer, to know what all that romantic scenery did to human beings who had to pull boats against the raging currents. The social conscience of China travelers was not usually their strong point. Yet a few did realize and cared what the Chinese felt, and they tried, each in his own way, to alleviate the suffering in these terminal dynastic years.

Among the most graphic descriptions of the famine of the late 1870's are those found in a little-known book titled *Wanderings in China,* by Constance F. Gordon-Cumming, published in 1886. One passage describes North China after some years of rainless summers and the spread of famine and disease through the land: "As Tien-tsin was the port at which the grain supplies for relief purposes were landed, thence to be forwarded to the famine districts, a multitude of miserable, starved wretches crowded hither, as many as a hundred thousand persons finding shelter in improvised hovels made of mud and straw. . . . In many of the famine villages a virulent form of typhus fever broke out, and fastening on victims already weakened to the utmost, found them such easy prey that from four to six hundred deaths in a night was no unusual occurrence.

"Although the corn-sacks . . . lay piled in vast heaps all along the shore, the difficulties of transporting these inland wellnigh baffled the authorities. Wherever it was possible to use water transport this was . . . done, and every stream and canal was crowded with grain boats; but where land-transport was necessary, then indeed trouble began. Every cart and every animal . . . was impressed into the service, but multitudes had already been killed for food. . . . Vast caravans were started across the plains, and across mountain ranges where the difficulties . . . were increased by the danger of attack by hill-tribes whom hunger had rendered desperate.

"The idea of employing these starving millions on making and repairing the roads never seems to have occurred to the authorities, so . . . carts were

broken and precious stores of grain were lost; men and beasts alike sank down to rise no more, and fell an easy prey to ravenous wolves, wild dogs, and birds of prey; so that the tracks were soon defined by the multitude of bleaching skeletons, varied in places by a cheerful exhibition of the heads of decapitated murderers and robbers.

"One man, with face blackened by starvation, told me how he alone survived from a family of sixteen. . . . Pitiful mothers drowned their children, or smothered them beneath the deep snow, and then put an end to their own miseries. . . . In every village a brooding silence told of the stupified misery of those who, still living, were only awaiting death. . . . Cannibalism, which at first stole in *sub rosa* . . . soon gained ground. . . . At last butchers' shops openly trafficked in this—the only available—food. . . .

"By January 1878 the names of upwards of eight millions of persons were entered on the books of the relief committee as being absolutely destitute. In May 1878 it was calculated that five millions . . . had actually died of starvation. . . ."

In these last years of the century, and in the bitter decades to come, the chasm between a bare living and starvation was to open ever more frequently, and resentment of the for-

eigners grew in many a thoughtful Chinese mind. Wang T'ao, a literary Chinese who worked with missionaries Medhurst and Dr. James Legge, and also with Sir Thomas Wade, later British Minister in Peking, voices his sense of humiliation and anger at his treatment even by these three mild and pleasant men, and, by extension, at all foreigners in China:

"These foreigners are not patient enough to learn Chinese thoroughly. As soon as they know the meaning of a few characters, they want to start writing books. . . . When you look at the foreigners with their high noses and deep-set eyes, you can sense how crafty they are. They treat all Chinese very shabbily, and they make their house servants work like animals without the slightest pity. They despise people of education like ourselves and never bother to show us the least courtesy. That they can find Chinese to work for them at all (and of course we only do it when we have no other way of getting a living) just goes to show how desperately poor the country is. And for this, of course, the foreigners despise China even more, while Chinese gentlemen find they have no alternative to putting up with this contempt. As for those Chinese who have to get their living from foreigners in this way, it is no doubt true that not one of them is a

A. Foreign militia in China (1900): (top) Japanese soldiers in the Engineer Corps. (middle) Russian soldiers. (bottom) Italian sharpshooters.
B. "Miracle in a Teapot," a Russian cartoon of the Chinese reaction to Western interventionist policies. Within the pot, ready for action, are soldiers from Germany, Russia, England, France, America and Japan.
C. A Chinese Boxer in full costume. Originally called the "Righteous and Harmonious Fists," the Boxers became the "Righteous and Harmonious Militia."
D. Execution by garroting.

man of very strong character, but at least there are among them people of talent who find themselves in such circumstances through no fault of their own." The short biography of Wang T'ao by the late Professor Henry McAleavy is a good introduction to the thoughts of literate Chinese in general about the ever-increasing depredations of the West in their country.

Even the violent eruption of xenophobic sentiment that resulted in a massacre of Westerners and their Chinese employees at Tientsin in 1870, the beginning of what historian H. B. Morse called "a legacy of bitter feelings," did little if anything to improve the behavior of Westerners in China. The French had foolishly built a cathedral on the site of an imperial temple at Tientsin in 1869. "It is not too much to say," Morse noted, "that . . . the French nation and French . . . missionaries were detested." The populace destroyed the hospital and the cathedral, massacring the vitriolic French consul, two priests, ten sisters and many Chinese employees of the French. The foreign reaction was to send the usual posse of gunboats and exact a hugh indemnity in money.

Among later and more highly placed scholars than Wang T'ao there began a movement for reform that was a follow-up to the rather ineffectual "self-strengthening movement." The Empress Dowager Tz'u-hsi had for the time being retired to the background, and the young Emperor Kuang-hsü reigned. His acceptance of the contents of the reform documents handed to him by one group of scholars, who saw what they thought would take their country out of the miseries it suffered at the hands of a corrupt government and a demanding West, was followed by a stream of reform decrees issued from the palace in the summer of 1898.

But the real power lay with the Empress Dowager, and she swiftly used it—canceling all but one of the decrees and having the emperor held prisoner for the rest of his life, while she took over once again her malign administration of China's destinies.

Greater movements than the gentlemen's reform movement were near. The so-called Boxers, of growing popularity among the mass of the Chinese in the north, began to rise up, their aims to "drive the foreigners into the sea, and to overthrow the Manchu dynasty." Later they dropped the anti-Manchu stance and, in the famous siege of the legations at Peking in 1900, were joined by the imperial armies at the command of the Empress Dowager. It is interesting that the real fury of the Boxers, and Chinese in general at that time, was vented not so much on the foreigners in the legations as on the Christian missionaries and their converts. In the countryside it was missionaries and Chinese Christians who were murdered before and during the height of the rebellion; in Peking it was the Roman Catholic cathedral that suffered the full fury of the Boxer braves.

Peking was once again taken by an allied force, and the court fled in disguise southwest to the old capital of Sian. Before they withdrew, Peking was looted by Boxers and Chinese alike. Historian Morse recorded something of the aftermath: "Peking was humbled in the dust . . . and suffered as Asiatic cities have always suffered when taken by assault by Asiatic armies—but now the invading forces were the armies of the Western powers. Strong men fled: those not so strong fled if they could find the means of transport, but that was scanty; many of the Manchu nobility and countless thousands of women put an end to their lives; many men were killed in a wild orgy of slaughter; the survivors who remained cowered like whipped hounds in their kennels." The Boxers and Chinese imperial troops had plundered, "but they had only skimmed the surface. The foreign troops now set to work to sack it riotously, but systematically. At first they spread over the city . . . wherever their fancy led them; then each contingent plundered the district assigned to it. . . ."

For the Chinese, the orgy of mayhem in their capital and in other northern places merely proved once more that the defenders of the twin Western faiths, Christian and mercantile, were unjust and barbarous, and that their preaching of justice to all men was a sham which they cast aside at will. On the other hand, many Chinese saw the Boxers, whatever their excesses, as a patriotic movement dedicated to what many Chinese except those in foreign employ thought to be the most desirable thing—the driving of the foreigners into the sea.

"The empire," wrote Morse, "was humiliated as it had never been from any of its previous wars, for it had lost, not only prestige, but reputation as well. . . . [It] was now called upon to enter on a diplomatic battle, as a result of which the nation was subjected to even deeper abasement."

The echoes of that T'ang dynasty emperor's words resound back and forth over the whole Boxer episode, 1,100 years after he determined "to dry up this vile source of errors which flood the empire . . . so that in the customs of our people there shall be no mixture."

Within a decade of the humiliation of 1900, and despite a reform movement much more radical than that envisaged by the emperor in 1898, belatedly introduced by the Empress Dowager, the old order perished.

The Empress Dowager's death in 1908 (preceded one day by that of the emperor, whom she probably had murdered) left, at her command, an even more unfortunate male on the throne — Henry Pu-yi, a child who was in turn to become a Japanese puppet in the state of Manchukuo in northeastern China and after that to fall prisoner to the Russians, to be repatriated to China and imprisoned by the Communists until finally he emerged as an old man and an ordinary citizen. The regent during Pu-yi's brief reign was Prince Ch'un, a man who with other equally ignorant and arrogant Manchu leaders attempted with total lack of success to stem the tide of new thinking in China and to fossilize (or refossilize) the old regime.

The complex process of change had begun for a 2,000-year-old way of life and government, and there was no reversing it—however excruciating and protracted the transformation might be. The revolution that set up the republic of Dr. Sun Yat-sen in 1912 was not, in fact, a revolution but a radical

reform movement. Little hope could be placed in a government always weak, only now and then supported by armed force of a magnitude that permitted it to execute its program, and frequently not in control of more than parts of the country. The several Western powers in China all jockeyed for position with various opposing factions and armies of the warlords, who virtually ruled China in these years, each of them trying to back the eventual winner. The warlords tore China apart. Ruthless commanders at the head of rabble armies equipped with guns of this or that Western power rampaged hither and thither across China, eating the scarce food of the people, looting, raping, burning—in what, for ordinary people, was an apparently endless time of agony.

In the cities and towns the old rule of the scholar-gentry, mild by comparison, was taken over by the most ruthless businessmen, Chinese and Western alike. The conditions of the work force in the great factories of Shanghai, Tientsin and Wuhan, to name the more prominent, were brutal in the extreme. It was as if, in an unconscious premonition of the end, the industrialists and others extracted the last ounce of toil from workers who otherwise would starve—as did so many millions of their fellow men.

The contemporary poet Feng Chih crystallized the urban scene in a few lines of a type of verse that was as new and (to the Chinese) as curious as the altered nondynastic state of China. In *Northern Wanderings* he wrote:

*Beastlike motor cars*
*Marauding in the streets,*
*Bony horses pulling broken carts,*
*Shrieking with their necks out-*
*stretched.*
*Jewish bankers, Greek restau-*
*rants,*
*Japanese drifters, White Russian*
*brothels,*
*All gather in this strange place**
*With complete complacency.*
*Rich Chinese merchants*
*With their fat smug smiles,*
*Concubines in outlandish foreign*
*clothes . . .*
*And prostitutes harboring poison-*
*ous germs*
*Gaudily strolling in the streets.*
*Am I wandering in hell?*
*Sinking deeper and deeper at*
*every step. . . .*

Wen I-to, a more profound poet, if not a prolific one, dug deeper through the surface of the society that was dominated by newly Westernized cities. In a remarkable poem titled "Dead Water," dating from the late 1920's, he summed up by analogy the seemingly hopeless state of China:

---
*Harbin, in the industrial northeast.

*This is a ditch of hopelessly dead*
*water.*
*No clear breeze can raise half a*
*ripple on it.*
*Why not throw in some rusty metal*
*scraps,*
*Or even some of your leftover food*
*and soup?*

*Perhaps the copper will turn its*
*green patina into jade,*
*And on the tin can rust will bloom*
*into peach blossoms;*
*Then let grease weave a layer of*
*silk brocade,*
*And germs brew out colored*
*clouds.*

. . . .

*This is a ditch of hopelessly dead*
*water,*
*A place where beauty can never*
*live.*
*Might as well let vice cultivate it,*
*And see what kind of a world it*
*can create.*

The republic failed because it could find no substitute for the old order that was strong enough to bring about the cohesion that a fragmented China required. Japan set up a state in the industrial northeast, and edged and infiltrated into China proper, slowly undermining whatever was vulnerable. With the rising power of the Communist party and its attempts to mobilize the people to fight the Japanese in-

vaders, and the general policy of the Kuomintang (Nationalist party) under Chiang Kai-shek to try merely to neutralize the Japanese, a chaotic situation arose which further injured the country. Drought and floods added their accents of horror. Millions fled from famine—into the arms of starvation in places that seemed to hold some hope but proved unable to support the influx.

It is almost impossible to exaggerate the appalling miseries of the Chinese in the years before World War II. Yet in these years the Chinese were slowly forming a new approach to life. It may in part be shown in the literary revolution that took place, exemplified by such men as Lu Hsün, Hu Shih and Kuo Mo-jo. Of the three, Lu Hsün was the most brilliant writer, and his short stories are classics that, though treating life in China, deal with mankind at large—and especially that vast segment of it which constitutes the underprivileged classes. An early story, "Diary of a Madman," deals with a man who suffers from a persecution complex. Or does he? The "madman" reads a book of history: "This history recorded no dates, but over every page were scrawled the words 'benevolence, righteousness, truth, virtue.'" Yet then the reader also sees "all over it in a succession of two words between the lines: 'Eat men!' " The comment is on traditional Chinese society, on Confucian benevolence that was a cloak for what Lu Hsün considered its underlying ruthless nature.

Not only were writers and poets turning away from the world of classical literature toward that of the people at large, and to the question of what would relieve China of all its miseries, but popular newspapers (new to China) and magazines sprang up by the hundreds, and a new climate of public opinion began to form.

And there were signs of change among Westerners. Bertrand Russell, in a book dating from 1922, writes in a manner that is unmistakably not that of the older school of "China hands": "When I went to China, I went to teach; but every day that I stayed I thought less and less of what I had to teach them and more of what I had to learn from them. . . . Among those whose stay is short, or who go only to make money, [this attitude] is sadly rare. It is rare because the Chinese do not excel in the things we really value—military prowess and industrial enterprise." Some other comments are equally penetrating. "The Chinese, from the highest to the lowest, have an imperturbable quiet dignity, which is not usually destroyed by a European education. . . . They admit China's weaknesses . . . but they do not consider efficiency in homicide the most important quality in a man or a nation. I think, at bottom, they think that China is the greatest nation in the world, and has the finest civilization. A Westerner cannot be expected to accept this view, because it is based on traditions utterly different from his own. But gradually one comes to feel that it is . . . not an absurd view."

Sufferance at the hands of the world such as the Chinese endured in the hundred and more years beginning with the opium confrontations left scars that cannot easily be effaced. But China, now, it seems, as in the past, asks little of that outer world except that it leave her unmolested so that she can pursue her own affairs in her own way. Here, Russell saw prophetically. The Chinese, he wrote, "are capable of wild excitement, often of a collective kind. . . . And it is this element in their character which makes them incalculable, and makes it impossible even to guess their future. One can imagine a section of them becoming fanatically Bolshevist, or anti-Japanese, or Christian, or devoted to some leader who would eventually declare himself Emperor." Though an overstatement, to be sure, history has proven these prophecies.

The final success of the Communist revolution in China, and the concomitant ending of the holocaust of national degradation, eventually came to pass. With those later events we are not here concerned. But a knowledge of the outline of that terminal century of Confucian dominance and its final eradication, and of the ever-increasing intervention of the West for its own purposes, is absolutely necessary in order to gain even the most superficial insight into the process by which the nation rose again at last to its own new form of greatness.

Nigel Cameron
Hong Kong
January 1978

# Chronology:
# The Last Dynasty
# & the Opening
# to the West

**1644** The Ch'ing dynasty is established in Peking by the Manchus.

**1662–1722** Reign of K'ang-hsi: successful consolidation of Manchu rule over China begins long era of peace and prosperity; Jesuit experts in Western science and technology are employed in the court.

**1736–95** Reign of Ch'ien-lung: the zenith of Ch'ing accomplishments and prosperity is attained but followed by governmental abuses and corruption; in the final years rapid population growth occurs.

**1793** Lord Macartney, sent by Britain to secure a more favorable trade arrangement and diplomatic ties, is received as a tribute bearer, his requests politely refused.

**1796–1804** The White Lotus Rebellion, the first major political disturbance in more than a century, ushers in an era of domestic strife that plagues China until the dynasty falls.

**1839–42** The First Opium War, results when Chinese authorities attempt to stop the flow of opium; ends with the first "unequal treaties," which give new status to Westerners and allow them free access to five treaty ports (including Canton) in addition to Hong Kong.

**1850–64** The Taiping Rebellion is instigated by members of the Hakka minority in South China; imbued with a pseudo-Christian ideology espousing primitive communal ideals, the movement has enormous appeal for millions of discontented Chinese; the uprising is finally suppressed by Chinese regional leaders, but not before several other widespread rebellions arise in response and great damage is sustained by the dynasty.

**1856–60** The Second Opium War, China's next major conflict with European military power: British and French armies force China to sign a new set of treaties that further erode Chinese sovereignty.

**1862–74** Reign of T'ung-chih: under the guidance of the Empress Dowager, Tz'u-hsi, the court supports a new policy of "self-strengthening," seeking to adopt Western devices and techniques for self-protection; great efforts are made to restore Confucian government as the expanded domestic rebellions are suppressed.

**1884–85** Sino-French War: resulting from French encroachment in Annam, one of China's tributary states; the conflict clearly indicates the ineffective leadership in Peking and suggests the failure of the self-strengthening campaign; as a result, China loses Annam.

**1894–95** Sino-Japanese War: Another lost war, now at the hands of the Japanese (pejoratively labeled "Dwarfs" by the Chinese) convinces many of the scholarly elite that a weakened China was soon to be torn apart by the foreign powers; China loses Taiwan, as well as her influence over Korea and Liu-ch'iu (the Ryukyu Islands).

**1898** Hundred Days' Reform: in a desperate attempt to forestall the partitioning of China, the court sponsors radical change as directed by K'ang Yu-wei. Supported by conservatives, the Empress Dowager returns from retirement to lead a coup against her nephew, the emperor, who is placed under house arrest for the rest of his life.

**1900** Boxer Uprising: the Empress Dowager and court xenophobes allow the Boxers, an anti-foreign secret society, to attack the legations in Peking; many missionaries and other Westerners, as well as thousands of Chinese Christians are killed before Peking falls to the allied force of eight nations; by labeling the episode a "rebellion," the foreign powers allow the mortally wounded dynasty to survive.

**1908** Deaths of the Empress Dowager and Emperor Kuang-hsü.

**1911** Wu-ch'ang Uprising: Led by followers of Sun Yat-sen on October 10, the incident marks the beginning of the Republican Revolution.

**1912** The last Ch'ing emperor, a child, is forced to relinquish the throne; a weak republican government, dominated by old-style military figures, replaces the dynasty.

H. C. White: Cliff of the Virgin Fairy, Fairy Cave Temples, southern Chekiang, c1925.

# Pioneer Photographers

The first known Western photographer in China was a man named Felice A. Beato. Like Marco Polo, who traveled before him in that land which remained mysterious to the rest of the world until our own times, Beato was a Venetian. He had been employed as an assistant to the superintendent and chief engraver at the Constantinople Imperial Mint, and it was with his superior officer there, James Robertson, that he went to the Crimean peninsula. Robertson, a photographer and engraver, recorded the aftermath of several of the terrible events of the war, after which he and Beato worked on a series of photographs of Constantinople, Athens, Malta, Cairo and the biblical sites of Palestine which they had begun earlier. Then news of the Indian Mutiny seems to have impelled them to take ship for India, where they recorded the evidences of that disastrous chain of events. The prints made from their photographs in India were produced by the oldest photographic company in the subcontinent—Shepherd's, founded in the hill station of Simla in 1843.

Robertson elected to stay on in India and to join Shepherd's, while the younger Beato, apparently—from the little we know of his actual life—remained filled with the spirit of adventure, and proceeded farther east to photograph the dastardly goings-on in the terminal phases of the Second Opium War in China. Beato went on with the armies in that fateful year, 1860, to the capture of Tientsin and the sacking of the Imperial Summer Palace outside the capital, Peking, which had been occupied.

While Robertson used the albumen-on-glass process invented by C. Niepce de St. Victor in which light-sensitive salts of silver are held in suspension in albumen while forming a coating on a glass sheet, Beato in China was using a newer development in photographic processes—the collodion plate invented in 1848 by F. Scott Archer. In this process the silver salts sensitive to light are held in finely separated suspension in a solution of soluble halides containing gelatin.

Several factors involved in the taking of a photograph in these early days make it astonishing that the attempt was ever undertaken except in the most ideal circumstances. First, the cameras had to be large in order to contain glass plates of 10 x 12 inches, or 12 x 16, or even larger. The weight of the glass plates, which had to be carried, securely packed in wooden boxes, was a formidable obstacle in itself. Generally, the camera had several heavy interchangeable lenses. The tripod resembled a primitive version of that stout and burdensome tripod used today for such instruments as the surveyor's theodolite. In addition, some form of portable darkroom had to be taken along, to include a lightproof tent, all the chemicals for coating the plates with collodion emulsion and airtight glass jars for developing and fixing. It is not surprising to hear of photographers hiring a small army of local porters to trek over the country so that they could set up their clumsy laboratories in the field and, with an intense exertion that can only be imagined, take their photographs.

In those days the sensitive wet coating on the glass plate was slow to react to light, and exposures were commensurately long. Prints had to be made directly from the resulting negatives.

The photographer of the nineteenth century—right up to 1899, when Eastman introduced the first celluloid film coated with silver bromide emulsion—had to be a person of considerable stamina and extensive training in chemistry and its practical applications, making his own emulsion, developing and printing with what were, by any standard, somewhat primitive materials. Each picture was the hard-won result of an endurance test in which numerous things could go wrong: a puff of wind as the wet plate was being loaded could spray it with all manner of particles (dust, straw, leaves, sand, depending on the location); a stumbling donkey on a foreign trail could wreck a couple of boxes of glass plates or already prepared negatives.

John Thomson, who arrived in China in 1868, tells an amusing story which illustrates yet another hazard of photography, one that continued long after the wet and the dry plates were superseded by Eastman and even by color film: the objections of the subjects at whom the lens was pointed.

"This bridge over the river Han at Chaochow is perhaps one of the most remarkable in China. Like old London Bridge . . . it affords space for one of the city markets. . . . While taking the illustration, I endeavored to avoid the crowd by starting to work at daybreak, but the people were astir, and seeing my strange instrument pointed cannonwise towards their shaky dwellings, they at once decided I was practising some outlandish witchcraft against the old bridge and its inhabitants. The market stalls were abandoned, that the barbarian who had come to brew mischief for them might be properly pelted. The roughs and the market people came heart and soul to the task, armed with mud and missiles, which were very soon flying in a shower above my head. I made a plunge for the boat and once on board, it told to my advantage when I charged a ruffian with the pointed tripod as he attempted a black eye of mud in exchange. For myself I sustained but little damage, while it may fairly be said that the bridge was taken at the point of the tripod."

John Thomson had a sense of humor. He was also excellent at reporting on emulsion *la condition humaine*, which he proved not only in China but in London streets, in Southeast Asia and elsewhere.

Thomson was born in Edinburgh in 1837, and as a young man had some reputation there as a photographer of architecture. But little enough seems to be known of him before he set out on his first foreign trip. Two Edinburgh men, Robert Adamson and David Octavius Hill, were important in the history of photography in at least two respects. Doubtless, Thomson knew their work. They achieved a higher emulsion speed than was possible in the calotype process, using paper impregnated with silver iodide that had been invented by Henry Fox Talbot in England about 1840, and they revolutionized photography by using the camera in the open air as well as in the studio.

We do not know whether John

Thomson ever saw any of the photographs of Felice Beato of the East, but it is quite possible. And it could have been Beato's photographs—or indeed just a spirit of adventure not uncommon in young men—which made him decide on the long sea voyage eastward. His first travels were fairly brief, cut short by illness in Cambodia and Malaysia. He returned home and four years after starting on that first eastward trip set out again, settling in Penang and adjacent areas for some months, then starting a photographic studio in Singapore. A restless need to travel and to photograph seems to have been strong in him, and later that same year, 1865, he was on his way to Thailand and Cambodia. By 1868 he had reached Hong Kong—his jumping-off ground for China, where he was to travel, on his own estimate, between four and five thousand miles. Explaining his intention in the book he published later in four volumes, *Illustrations of China and Its People*, which has 200 photographs and cost the large (at that time) sum of £12 sterling, Thomson remarked: "I feel somewhat sanguine about the success of the undertaking, and I hope to see the process which I have thus applied adopted by other travelers; for the faithfullness of the pictures [as opposed to engravings from photographs which were the norm of the time] affords the nearest approach that can be made towards placing the reader actually before the scene which is represented."

This was precisely the point. The novel experience of being "placed before" the astonishing and to most people utterly unknown scenes of Chinese life and country ensured the success of the book, but adding to its success was the earnest textual matter that Thomson included. It was "compiled from information derived from the most trustworthy sources," as well as from his own notes made during his more than four years in China. Unfortunately, there were few "trustworthy sources" on all particulars of what Thomson photographed, and they were even less trustworthy on philosophical and historical matters.

Thomson's travels in China were ambitious for the period. From Hong Kong he went to Canton and inland for a while; then back to the coast and over to Formosa; then back to Swatow on the South China coast, up to Amoy and to Foochow, from there making an inland excursion into Fukien province, where "the river Min will here afford examples of the grand mountain scenery . . . and will form an attractive portion of the work, as the great artery which carries an annual supply of about seventy million pounds of tea to the Foochow market"—some of it destined for his readers' cups. Then to Shanghai, where he contrasts what he sees as an English city with "native dwellings huddled together, as if pressed back to make way for the higher civilization that has planted a city in their midst."

Thomson was fascinated by Ningpo, and its Snowy Valley with its celebrated azaleas, "its mountain scenery, its cascades and waterfalls," are specifically mentioned and photographed. From there up the not long opened Yangtze, with its "weird scenery of the gorges," and on north, coastwise via other treaty ports to Peking: "The remarkable antiquities, the palace, temples, and observatory; the different races in the great metropolis; the ruins of the Summer Palace and the Ming Tombs. . . . After which I will guide the reader through the Nankow Pass, and take my leave of him at the Great Wall."

The impact of such a documentation in Thomson's day is rather hard to imagine now. His exotic China was later matched by his photographs of the slums of London, then almost equally unknown to the genteel reader of books. With a proven genius for sympathetic documentation, John Thomson was truly a photographic pioneer.

Of all the photographers who ventured far into China, perhaps Ernest Henry "Chinese" Wilson was the most thorough in his field, the most persevering in the face of difficulty and danger. He was a botanist, and his first visits to China were made in 1899 and 1903 with the Veitch expeditions. On these journeys he carried what is described as a "snapshot camera," but he was better equipped in 1906, when sent by the director of the Arnold Arboretum and urged to take along a camera capable of taking plates of 8½ x 6½ as well.

Wilson should be viewed as an accomplished photographer, and his general scholarship permitted him to write well of his travels. His book *A Naturalist in Western China* tells us something, modestly, of the hardships of travel and photography in the remoter parts of China in those days. Far up the long arm of the Yangtze—at Ichang, where cargoes had to be transshipped to other vessels to pass the rapids and reach the upper river cities, Wilson began his exploration in search of all manner of unknown species of plant and tree, as well as local Chinese variants of known ones. They lived roughly, sleeping in miserable little village inns, daring the various bandits who infested parts of China at that time.

For the Arboretum journeys he took with him a small roll-film camera for personal use, and a Sanderson whole-plate camera and equipment in three heavy boxes. This type of instrument was even then becoming outdated, but it had the advantages of allowing accurate composition on the big ground-glass screen and of not distorting the perspective of tall objects.

Wilson's total of 5,000 glass plate photographs for the Arboretum are only about half of his prodigious output, for he took approximately the same number of nitrate-base negatives for his own uses. Carefully not expending his material too rapidly on outward journeys, he was at pains to use it up on return trips so that nothing would be wasted. On successive journeys he often went back to the exact locations he had previously visited, photographing the same trees and, of course, collecting seeds and cuttings.

One of his problems was movement: the emulsion speeds of those days did not permit accurate rendering of moving objects, and patience and devotion to the aim in view were necessary to get a picture of some great tree at a moment when the lighting was right and when the breeze was not swaying its branches. Considering this factor alone, apart from the hazards of the actual expeditions, Wilson's work must be seen as herculean.

There were many excellent amateur photographers in China after 1860, and many more after the invention of the dry plate and eventually celluloid film and the more or less pocket-size bellows camera. One finds thousands of their photographs, of extreme interest to the historian, scattered liberally throughout the books written in those times. Most are documentary, dealing with the landscape and architecture of many parts of China, less often with people until the availability of faster emulsions. A select few, many of which can be found in this volume, are imbued with mastery and artfulness.

About those hundreds of ardent photographers in China of the late nineteenth and early twentieth centuries little enough is known. Writers who took their own photographs abounded—Mrs. Archibald Little was but one example, an ardent anti-footbinding campaigner who also used photographs by others, in some cases her friends, to illustrate her bulky books. And, of course, photographic studios sprang up in Peking and in other centers of population.

One among several about whom there is some surviving knowledge is John Henry Hinton, born in London in 1875. During his apprenticeship to a piano tuner with a well-known musical instrument company, he bought technical photographic manuals which doubtless started him off in photography.

Hinton's employers received a call for a young man to work in the Shanghai office of Samuel Moutrie and Company—a music firm which still exists in Hong Kong—and Hinton was chosen. In 1894 he left for China, where he not only had considerable mobility but also the services of a Chinese translator. Together they traveled for two years while Hinton learned Chinese and something of Chinese culture. In the oldest surviving album of his photographs, fourteen are from China—views of Shanghai and pictures of friends.

When the Allied forces arrived in Tientsin in 1898, Hinton volunteered to accompany them to Peking. One album dated November 2, 1901, contains photographs of ruins and army movements in Peking and Tientsin. The following year Hinton photographed the return to Peking from Sian of the Empress Dowager, but only a single plate and twenty-two contact print-out paper proofs remain from this episode.

During his years in China until he left in 1914, Hinton traveled exten-sively, to Hong Kong and Ningpo, up the Yangtze to numerous ports on that long river and beyond China to Singapore.

Beato, Thomson, Hinton and Wilson were pioneers. There were certainly many more. We know some of their photographs from the books that were illustrated by examples of their work, but we seldom know much else.

In considering the totality of photographs from those now far-off days, several aspects must strike the viewer. One that has not been much discussed is that virtually all the photographs were taken by Westerners and many reflect (if they reflect any view at all) a Western attitude to the scenes and people they depict.

Naturally, too, the photographs are colored by Western social attitudes in regard to the Chinese. The "quaint" and the gruesome, the "picturesque" poverty of many Chinese in the late Ch'ing dynasty, the little-understood but fascinating architecture in town and in country, the "curious" handicrafts, and sometimes the adulation of much that was worst in Chinese art to the exclusion of what was great—are all aspects richly documented, just as their equivalents are in other "foreign" places.

The China of those Western photographers—the handful of profes-sionals and the multitude of amateurs—is a China that, in the days before the Communist government transformed the rural and urban face of that immense land, was at once familiar and unfamiliar. The familiar part was the scenery and the architecture. But the strange and somehow disquieting aspect was the people. For, after the end of World War II, no sensible Westerner could take the attitude that formerly prevailed toward the Chinese people. There was the inescapable knowledge that the West was no longer the master of the East.

It is with such considerations in mind that the photographs of old China must be looked at, a fascinating view from a Western perspective.

N.C.

# Sources

*It is fortunate that the early photographers included in this volume understood that China was a special land to be approached with respect and open eyes. The finest results of their labor provide rare glimpses of a life that would soon be radically altered. Beyond record or document, a powerful presence is evoked, extending our sense of life as well as the ebb and flow of events in China.*

*With few exceptions the pioneer photographers did not identify their pictures. In many cases we do not even know the photographer's name. This necessitated filling in great gaps when we began to write captions. By searching through published records and by checking other contemporary photographs, we are able to pin down some details of persons, places and events that might render the collection more meaningful. In the main, however, we were forced to agree with an old Chinese proverb: "One picture is worth ten thousand words."*

Fred W. Drake,
Associate Professor
of Chinese History,
University of Massachusetts

## Photographs

Cover: Photographer unknown: Merchant and daughters with servant, c1875, Bibliothèque Nationale, Paris.
Page 2: Library of Congress, Washington, D.C.
12: Graphics International, Washington, D.C.
13: The Arnold Arboretum, Harvard University.
14: Howard Ricketts Collection, London.   15: Freer Gallery of Art, Washington, D.C.   16–17: Essex Institute, Frederick T. Ward China Library, Salem, Mass.   18: Bibliothèque Nationale, Paris.

19: Stuart Collection, Rare Book Division, New York Public Library, Astor, Lenox and Tilden Foundation.   20: Freer Gallery of Art, Washington, D.C.   21: Stuart Collection, Rare Book Division, New York Public Library, Astor, Lenox and Tilden Foundation.   22: Daniel Wolf Collection, New York City.   23: Howard Ricketts Collection, London.   24: Arnold H. Crane Collection, Chicago.   25: Essex Institute, Frederick T. Ward China Library, Salem, Mass.   26: The Arnold Arboretum, Harvard University.   27: Library of Congress, Washington, D.C.   28: The Arnold Arboretum, Harvard University.   29: Essex Institute, Frederick T. Ward China Library, Salem, Mass.   30: Chaoying Fang.   31: Essex Institute, Frederick T. Ward China Library, Salem, Mass.   32: Chaoying Fang.   33: Graphics International, Washington, D.C.   34: Library of Congress, Washington, D.C.   35: The National Archives, Washington, D.C.   36–37: Hillelson/Kahn Collection, London.   38, 39: The Arnold Arboretum, Harvard University.   40: Essex Institute, Frederick T. Ward China Library, Salem, Mass.   41: Library of Congress, Washington, D.C.   42: Howard Ricketts Collection, London.   43: Daniel Wolf Collection, New York City.   44: National Army Museum, London.   45: Graphics International, Washington, D.C.   46: Stuart Collection, Rare Book Division, New York Public Library, Astor, Lenox and Tilden Foundation.   47, 48: Daniel Wolf Collection, New York City.   49: Essex Institute, Frederick T. Ward China Library, Salem, Mass.   50, 51: Library of Congress, Washington, D.C.   52: Essex Institute, Frederick T. Ward China Library, Salem, Mass.   53: Daniel Wolf Collection, New York City.   54: Freer Gallery of Art, Washington, D.C.   55: Library of Congress, Washington, D.C.   56: Essex Institute, Frederick T. Ward China Library, Salem, Mass.   57, 58: Daniel Wolf Collection, New York City.   59: Library of Congress, Washington, D.C.   60: Elaine Ellman Collection, New York City.   61: Stuart Collection, Rare Book Division, New York Public Library, Astor, Lenox and Tilden Foundation.   62, 63: Museum of Mankind, Trustees of the British Museum, London.   64: Chaoying Fang.   65, 66–67: Stuart Collection, Rare Book

Division, New York Public Library, Astor, Lenox and Tilden Foundation. 68: Chaoying Fang. 69: Peabody Museum, Salem, Mass. 70: Victoria & Albert Museum, London. 71: Essex Institute, Frederick T. Ward China Library, Salem, Mass. 72, 73, 74, 75: Library of Congress, Washington, D.C. 76, 77: The Arnold Arboretum, Harvard University. 78: Smithsonian Institution, Washington, D.C. 79: Graphics International, Washington, D.C. 80: Stuart Collection, Rare Book Division, New York Public Library, Astor, Lenox and Tilden Foundation. 81: Howard Ricketts Collection, London. 82: Daniel Wolf Collection, New York City. 83: Library of Congress, Washington, D.C. 84: Daniel Wolf Collection, New York City. 85: Essex Institute, Frederick T. Ward China Library, Salem, Mass. 86: Bibliothèque Nationale, Paris. 87: Pontifico Foreign Missions Institute, Milan. 88: *China Yesterday & Today,* Thomas Crowell, 1927. 89, 90: Smithsonian Institution, Washington, D.C. 91: Daniel Wolf Collection, New York City. 92: Library of Congress, Washington, D.C. 93: International Museum of Photography at George Eastman House, Rochester, N.Y. 94: Essex Institute, Frederick T. Ward China Library, Salem, Mass. 95: Daniel Wolf Collection, New York City. 96: Library of Congress, Washington, D.C. 97: Stuart Collection, Rare Book Division, New York Public Library, Astor, Lenox and Tilden Foundation. 98: Library of Congress, Washington, D.C. 99: National Army Museum, London. 100: Naval Historical Center, Washington, D.C., U.S. Navy, Collection of Rear Admiral Ammen C. Farenholt, N.S.N. (M.C.). 101: Library of Congress, Washington, D.C. 102: Howard Ricketts Collection, London. 103: Daniel Wolf Collection, New York City. 104: Arnold H. Crane Collection, Chicago. 105: The Arnold Arboretum, Harvard University. 106: Museum of New Mexico, Santa Fe. 107: Peabody Museum, Salem, Mass. 108: Stuart Collection, Rare Book Division, New York Public Library, Astor, Lenox and Tilden Foundation. 109: Museum of New Mexico, Santa Fe. 110: Bibliothèque Nationale, Paris. 111: Graphics International, Washington, D.C. 112: Museum of Fine Arts, Boston. 113: Victoria & Albert

Museum, London. 114: Daniel Wolf Collection, New York City. 115: Essex Institute, Frederick T. Ward China Library, Salem, Mass. 116: Chaoying Fang. 117: Essex Institute, Frederick T. Ward China Library, Salem, Mass. 118: Peabody Museum, Salem, Mass. 119: Essex Institute, Frederick T. Ward China Library, Salem, Mass. 120: Elaine Ellman Collection, New York City. 121: Peabody Museum, Salem, Mass. 122: Hinton Family Collection; Edmonton Art Gallery, Alberta, Canada. 123, 124: Essex Institute, Frederick T. Ward China Library, Salem, Mass. 125: Arnold H. Crane Collection, Chicago. 150: Museum of Fine Arts, Boston. 159: Library of Congress, Washington, D.C.
End papers: Photographer unknown: Ming tombs, Nanking, c1865, Peabody Museum, Salem, Mass. Back cover: Photographer unknown: Guardian at temple gate, c1875, Bibliothèque Nationale, Paris.

## Illustrations

Page 127: New York Public Library Picture Collection (A,D,E); *The Rise of Modern China,* Immanuel C. Y. Hsü, Oxford University Press, 1970 (B,C). 130: Library of Congress, Washington, D.C. (A,B); New York Public Library Picture Collection (C,D). 134: Essex Institute, Frederick T. Ward China Library, Salem, Mass. (A); *The Oriental Adventure,* Timothy Severin, Little, Brown, 1976 (B); *Barbarians and Mandarins,* Nigel Cameron, John Weatherhill, 1970 (C,D,E). 137: *Barbarians and Mandarins,* Nigel Cameron, John Weatherhill, 1970 (A); New York Public Library Picture Collection (B,D); Library of Congress, Washington, D.C. (C); National Army Museum, London (E,F). 144: The National Archives, Washington, D.C. (A,C); *Peasant Revolts in China 1840–1949,* Jean Chesneaux, W. W. Norton, 1973 (B); Library of Congress, Washington, D.C. (D).

## Quotations

Page 12: *A Journey from St. Petersburg to Pekin,* 1719–22; *Illustrations of China and Its People,* Samson, Low, 1874. 25: *Diary,* Harvard University, 1949; inscription on painting, 1372; *idem.* 26: *Oriental Rambles,* published by the author, 1906; *A Chinese Childhood,* Methuen & Co., 1940; *China Opened,* 1838. 39: *Acta Orientalia,* trans. J. J. L. Duyrendak, Lugduni Batavorum, 1924; 1870. 40: *My Boy Chang; A Journey from St. Petersburg to Pekin,* 1719–22; Ida Pruitt, *A Daughter of Han,* Stanford University, 1967; provincial Chinese rhyme. 55: *Intimate China,* Hutchinson & Co., 1901. 56: *Wanderings in China,* 1886; *Gleanings from Fifty Years in China.* 72: *The New China,* Dodd, Mead, 1912; *Diary,* Harvard University, 1949; *In the Land of the Laughing Buddha — the Adventures of an American Barbarian in China,* 1924. 87: 1872; 1923; *Memorial to the Throne,* June 2, 1863. 88: *In the Land of the Laughing Buddha: The Adventures of an American Barbarian in China,* 1924; compiled by Laura C. Holloway, Funk & Wagnalls, 1885; *Memorial to the Throne,* December 27, 1863. 96: *Intimate China,* Hutchinson & Co., 1901; from translation by Fortunato Prandi, 1849. 113: Quoted in Theodore Walrond, *Letters and Journals, Eighth Earl of Britain,* 1873; *The Attaché of Peking,* 1900. 124: *Lion and Dragon in Northern China,* 1910; *The First Chapter of Spring,* 1920.

# Acknowledgments

*Great appreciation is extended to the following, who made their photographic collections available and provided their services for the exhibition and this publication: Peter Chvany, Arnold Aboretum, Harvard University; Georges le Rider, Director, Claude Le Magny, curator, and Jean Pierre Seguin, Bibliothèque Nationale, Paris; Joyce Paulson, Boston Museum of Fine Arts; Douglas Clark, Edmonton Art Gallery, Alberta, Canada; Bryant*

*Tolles, Jr., Director Librarian, Robinson Murray III, Associate Librarian, and Marylou Birchmore, Administrative Assistant, Essex Institute, Salem, Massachusetts; John Samuels, Chairman of the Board, and Howard Kane, Assistant Vice President, Exchange National Bank, Chicago; Sarah Newmeyer, Slide Librarian, Freer Gallery of Art, Washington, D.C.; Mary Ann Margoles, George Eastman House, Rochester, New York; J. Beausoleil, Albert Kahn Collection, Departement des Hautes-de-Seine; Alan Fern, Director of Research Department, Leonard C. Faber, Assistant Exhibits Officer, and Sandra Shaffer Tinkham, Library of Congress, Washington, D.C.; Brian Durrans, Assistant Keeper, Museum of Mankind, British Museum, London; Susan Kismaric, Research Supervisor, The Museum of Modern Art, New York City; Arthur L. Olivas, Photographic Archivist, and Richard Rudisell, Curator, Museum of New Mexico, Santa Fe; James E. O'Neill, Acting Archivist of the United States, and Lee Scott Theisen, Exhibits Officer, National Archives, Washington, D.C.; Major Boris Mollo, Deputy Director, National Army Museum, London; Thomas Smith, Illustrations Editor, and Andrew Poggenpohl, Art Editor, National Geographic Magazine, Washington, D.C.; Herman Viola, Director, Smithsonian Institution, Washington, D.C.; Lawrence Murphy, Curator, Rare Book Division, and Julia van Hafften, Art and Architecture Department, New York Public Library; Peter Fetchko, Assistant Director, and Lucy J. Batcheldar, Curatorial Assistant in Ethnology, Peabody*

*Museum, Salem, Massachusetts; Rear Admiral John D. H. Kane, Jr., Director, and J. H. B. Smith, Captain U.S.N., Head Curator, Naval Historical Center, United States Department of the Navy, Washington, D.C.; Laurence Sickman, William Rockhill Nelson Gallery of Art, Atkins Museum of Fine Art, Kansas City, Missouri; Mark Haworth-Booth, Victoria & Albert Museum, London; Martha Smalley, Yale University Divinity Library.*

*Special thanks are extended to the following individuals for the diverse range of their assistance: Rocco Alberico; Helene Baltrusaitis, Fine Arts Officer, United States Information Service, Paris; Richard Benson; Stevie Bezencenet; Wendy Byrne; Nicholas Callaway, Director, Zabriskie Gallery, Paris; Peter Collins; Mary E. Fanette; Mrs. Sidney Gamble; John Garbarini; Philip Gefter; The Honorable Arthur A. Hartman, U.S. Ambassador to France; William Holman; Eikoe Hosoe; Christian Jussel; Roberta Kimmel-Cohn; Elisabeth Kramer; Gabriel Laderman; Jean Lee; Sal Lopes; Joel Snyder; Lynn Strong; Suzanne Wheeling; Ann Zeller.*

*Ian Fontein, Director of the Museum of Fine Arts, Boston, made incisive comments at the early stages of the photographic research, suggesting standards for image selection.*

*Nelson Ikon Wu, Edward Mallinkrodt Distinguished University Professor of Art and Chinese Culture, Washington University, St. Louis, in a brief meeting provided the publisher with a vital perspective on the photographs and an introduction to L. Carrington Goodrich.*

B. W. Kilburn: Scene along Yangtze River Gorges, c1900.